MEXICO

Michael D. Coe

MEXICO

Third edition, revised and enlarged

WITH 128 ILLUSTRATIONS

THAMES AND HUDSON

Ancient Peoples and Places
GENERAL EDITOR: GLYN DANIEL

Frontispiece: Monument 1 from San Lorenzo, Veracruz, a
Colossal Head in basalt. Olmec culture, Early Formative
period. Ht 2.84 m.

First published in Great Britain in 1962
by Thames and Hudson Ltd, London

Second edition published in the USA in 1982
by Thames and Hudson Inc., 500 Fifth Avenue,
New York, New York 10110
Third edition 1984
Reprinted 1986

Library of Congress Catalog Card Number 83-72968

Printed and bound in Great Britain

Contents

Foreword

The subject matter of this book is the story of the pre-Spanish peoples of Mexico, who with their neighbors the Maya were the most advanced of the American Indians. As it will be used here, the term 'Mexico' will mean all the land in that Republic which lies between the western border of the Maya civilization, and the northern frontier where Mexican farmers once met the nomadic tribesmen of the desert.

I have found it both feasible and justifiable to exclude the ancient Maya from this survey, although part of their territory was, in fact, within the boundaries of the present-day *Estados Unidos de México*. The Maya civilization of the Yucatan Peninsula and Central America was so extraordinarily complex that to do it justice would be impossible within the confines of the present volume. With a few notable exceptions, those remarkable people would appear to have remained within their own borders throughout the centuries; accordingly, other native cultures of the Republic can be considered quite independently without the problem of Maya influences seriously conflicting with the development of our theme. The latest revised edition of *The Maya*, the companion volume in the series, appeared in 1984 and should be read with it.

Some may be disappointed to find the Aztec empire confined to a single chapter. 'Aztec' and 'Mexico' seem almost synonymous, but we now know that in the total span of human occupation of that country, the Aztecs were late arrivals, their empire but a final and brilliant flicker before the light of native civilization was put out once and for all. Nevertheless, we know an enormous amount about the Aztecs, thanks to the accounts of Spanish friars and *conquistadores*, and to native and creole historians; archaeology has contributed disappointingly little to this fund of knowledge, with the exception of the brilliant new excavations in the remains of the Great Temple at Tenochtitlan, which was once the center of the Aztec empire.

A great deal of archaeological water has gone over the dam since *Mexico* first appeared in 1962, and since the revised edition of 1977. Some of this new research includes the Tehuacan Project directed by Richard S. MacNeish and now fully published; the search for Olmec origins and extensions, carried out by the Yale archaeological group at San Lorenzo Tenochtitlan, and by David C. Grove at the highland site of Chalcatzingo; the photogrammetric mapping of

Teotihuacan, the New World's largest city, by René Millon; the comprehensive study of the Valley of Oaxaca and the origins of Zapotec civilization by Kent V. Flannery and his associates; and the Great Temple project directed by Eduardo Matos M. The important settlement pattern surveys carried out by William Sanders and Jeffrey Parsons have thrown new light on the rise of civilized life in the Valleys of Mexico and Teotihuacan. Perhaps the most astonishing new body of data are the thoroughly Maya mural paintings uncovered of late in the state of Tlaxcala, several hundred miles from the Maya area proper. These and other new findings have been incorporated in the present volume.

A matter which must be touched upon is the pronunciation of the very formidable-looking words and names of ancient Mexico. Most of these are in Nahuatl, the national tongue of the Aztec state, and were transcribed in Roman letters in terms of the language spoken by the *conquistadores* of the sixteenth century. Thus, vowels and most consonants are generally pronounced as they would be in modern Spanish, with these exceptions:

x has the sound of the English *sh*, as it once had in Spanish
(witness the derivation of 'sherry' from the Spanish *Xerez*).
tl – this cluster is a voiceless surd consonant, much like
the Welsh *ll*

In Nahuatl, word stress always falls on the penultimate syllable. I have therefore omitted all accents in such words and names. However, various corruptions have crept into Nahuatl from Spanish, including occasional stress placed upon the final syllable (e.g., in many books, *Teotihuacán* is found in place of the more correct *Teotihuácan*).

I have used the correct Nahuatl form *Motecuhzoma* ('Angry Like a Lord') for the third and seventh Aztec kings; the familiar 'Montezuma' of numberless boyhood romances is hopelessly wrong and merely reflects the inability of most Spaniards to pronounce native names.

In recent years there have been important advances in the accurate correlation of dates derived from radiocarbon determinations with those of the Christian calendar. Dendrochronological studies of the bristlecone pine now suggest that before about 1000 BC there is an increasing deviation from 'true' dates back to a maximum of some 800 years at radiocarbon 4500 BC. No attempt has been made in this new edition to calibrate prehistoric dates with the 'true' dates from bristlecone pine, since there is still disagreement among specialists as to the correct calibration curve, and this curve itself only extends as far back as about 5000 BC. But readers who want a rough guide to 'true' prehistoric dates may find it helpful to bear in mind that a radiocarbon date of 1000 BC is in all probability 1200 BC in calendar years, radiocarbon 2000 BC is about 2500 BC, while radiocarbon 3000 BC would be approximately 3700 BC.

Many persons have aided me in the preparation of this book. *Mexico* had its inception as a volume in the Ancient Peoples and Places series thanks to the kind interest of the General Editor, Dr Glyn Daniel. I was introduced to him many years ago by our late friend, Geoffrey H. S. Bushnell, and I am still deeply grateful for the faith which both put in a young and completely unknown scholar. I have learned much from all those archaeologists whose work is mentioned in this book, but especially from personal friendship and close contact with Richard S. MacNeish, Richard A. Diehl, Kent V. Flannery, and David C. Grove. All those referred to in the List of Illustrations deserve my special thanks. I am also grateful to the Thames and Hudson staff for their help in enabling me to present often complex archaeological research to the general reader.

Chronological table

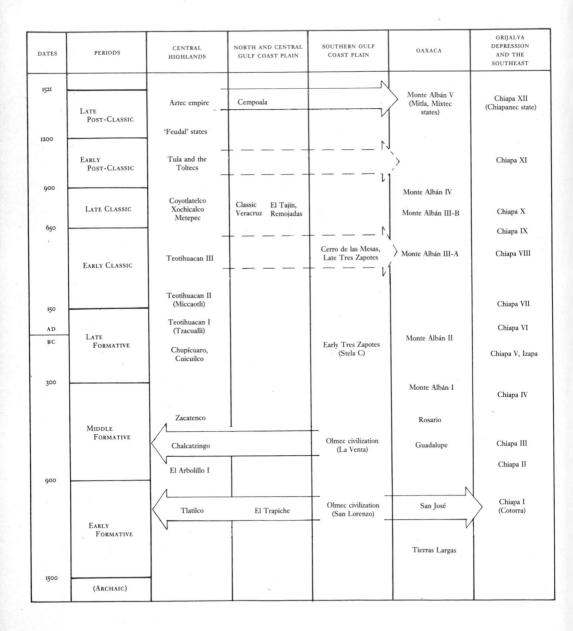

DATES	PERIODS	CENTRAL HIGHLANDS	NORTH AND CENTRAL GULF COAST PLAIN	SOUTHERN GULF COAST PLAIN	OAXACA	GRIJALVA DEPRESSION AND THE SOUTHEAST
1521		Aztec empire	Cempoala		Monte Albán V (Mitla, Mixtec states)	Chiapa XII (Chiapanec state)
	LATE POST-CLASSIC					
1200		'Feudal' states				
	EARLY POST-CLASSIC	Tula and the Toltecs				Chiapa XI
900					Monte Albán IV	
	LATE CLASSIC	Coyotlatelco Xochicalco Metepec	Classic Veracruz El Tajín, Remojadas		Monte Albán III-B	Chiapa X
650						Chiapa IX
	EARLY CLASSIC	Teotihuacan III		Cerro de las Mesas, Late Tres Zapotes	Monte Albán III-A	Chiapa VIII
150		Teotihuacan II (Miccaotli)				Chiapa VII
AD	LATE FORMATIVE	Teotihuacan I (Tzacualli)				Chiapa VI
BC		Chupícuaro, Cuicuilco		Early Tres Zapotes (Stela C)	Monte Albán II	Chiapa V, Izapa
300					Monte Albán I	Chiapa IV
	MIDDLE FORMATIVE	Zacatenco			Rosario	
		Chalcatzingo		Olmec civilization (La Venta)	Guadalupe	Chiapa III
		El Arbolillo I				Chiapa II
900	EARLY FORMATIVE	Tlatilco	El Trapiche	Olmec civilization (San Lorenzo)	San José	Chiapa I (Cotorra)
					Tierras Largas	
1500	(ARCHAIC)					

The ancient cultures of Mexico along with the Maya civilization comprise the larger entity known to archaeologists as 'Mesoamerica', a name first proposed by the anthropologist Paul Kirchhoff and including much of the great constriction that separates the masses of North and South America. Above all, the peoples of Mesoamerica were farmers, and had been somewhat isolated for thousands of years from the simpler cultivating societies of the American Southwest and Southeast by the desert wastes of northern Mexico, through which only semi-nomadic, hunting aborigines ranged in pre-Spanish times. Beyond the southeastern borders of Mesoamerica lay the petty chiefdoms of lower Central America, not distinguished by any achievements other than a high production of fine ceramics and quantities of jade or gold ornaments, lavishly heaped in the tombs of their great.

Further south yet, in Ecuador, Peru, and Bolivia, was the Andean area, most noted for its final glory, the immense Inca empire, but having native civilizations as far back in time as the tenth century before Christ, and large temple constructions even earlier than that. The Andean area and Mesoamerica were the twin peaks of American Indian cultural development, from which much else in the Western Hemisphere seems both peripheral and derived; yet this picture may be oversimplified, because recent research in the Pacific lowlands of Ecuador, the Caribbean coast of Colombia, and the upper reaches of the Amazon has shown that the important criteria of settled life – agriculture, pottery, and villages – may have had a precocious start in those areas.

Setting them off from the rest of the New World, the diverse cultures of Mesoamerica shared in a number of features most of which were pretty much confined to their area. The most distinctive of these is a complicated calendar based upon the permutation of a 260-day sacred cycle with the solar year of 365 days. Others are hieroglyphic writing (the Andean area never developed a script); bark-paper or deer-skin books which fold like screens; maps; an extensive knowledge of astronomy; a team game resembling basketball played in a special court with a solid rubber ball; large, well-organized markets and favored 'ports of trade'; chocolate beans as money; wars for the purpose of securing sacrificial victims; private confession, and penance by drawing blood from the ears, tongue, or penis; and a pantheon of extraordinary complexity.

1 Map of major topographical features of Mesoamerica.

Naturally, the peoples of Mesoamerica followed a number of other customs which are widespread among New World Indians, such as ceremonial tobacco smoking, but their typical method of food preparation as a unified complex appears to be unique. The basis of the diet was the triad of maize, beans, and squash. Maize was, and still is, prepared by soaking it overnight with lime, or boiling it with the same substance, then grinding it with a hand stone (Spanish *mano*) on a trough- or saddle-shaped quern (*metate*, from the Nahuatl *metlatl*). The resulting dough is either toasted by the housewife as flat cakes known in Spanish as *tortillas*, or else steamed or boiled as *tamales*. Always and everywhere in Mesoamerica, the hearth comprises three stones, and being the conceptual center of the world, is semi-sacred.

The geographic setting

On the map, Mexico resembles a great funnel, or rather, a cornucopia, with its widest part towards the north and its smallest end twisting to the south and east, meeting there the sudden expansion of the Maya area. There are few regions in the world with such a diverse geography as we find within this area – Mexico is not one, but many countries. All the climatic extremes of our globe are found, from arctic cold near the summits of the highest volcanoes to the Turkish-bath atmosphere of the coastal jungles. Merely to pass from one valley to another is to enter a markedly different ecological zone.

This variation would be of interest only to the tourist agencies if one neglected to consider the effect of these contrasts upon man's occupation of Mexico. A topsy-turvy landscape of this sort means a similar diversity of natural and cultivated products from region to region – above all, different crops with different harvest times. It means that no one region is now, or was in the past, truly self-sufficient. From the most remote antiquity, there has been an organic interdependence of one zone with the others, of one people or nation with all the rest. Thus, no matter how heterogeneous their languages or civilizations, the people of Mexico through exchange of products were bound up with each other symbiotically into a single line of development; for this reason, great new advances were registered throughout the land within quite brief intervals of time.

Most of this funnel-shaped country lies above 1,000 m, with really very little flat land. The Mexican highlands, our major concern in this book, are shaped by the mountain chains that swing down from the north, by the uplands between them, and by numerous volcanoes which have raised their peaks in fairly recent geological times. The western chain, the Sierra Madre Occidental, is the loftiest and broadest of these, being an extension of the Rocky Mountains; it and the Sierra Madre Oriental to the east enclose between their pine-clad ranges an immense inland plateau which is covered by mesquite-studded grasslands and occasionally even approaches true desert. Effectively outside the limits of Mesoamerican farming, the Mexican plateau was the homeland of barbarian hunters and collectors. As we move south, the two Sierras gradually

2 Central highlands of Mexico, near Puebla, with Popocatepetl volcano in the distance.

2

approach each other until the interior wastelands terminate some 300 miles north of the Valley of Mexico.

The Valley of Mexico, the center of the Aztec empire, is one of a number of natural basins in the midst of the Volcanic Cordillera, an extensive region of intense volcanism and frequent earthquakes. A mile and a half high with an area of 3,000 square miles, much of the Valley was once covered by a shallow lake of roughly figure-eight shape, now largely disappeared through ill-advised drainage and general desiccation of central Mexico in post-Conquest times. Since the Valley of Mexico has no natural outlet, changing rainfall patterns have produced severe fluctuations in the extent of the lake. As will be seen in Chapter 9, the Aztec table was amply supplied by foods raised on its swampy margins in the misnamed 'floating gardens', or *chinampas*. Surrounded by hills on all sides, the Valley is dominated on the southeast by the snowy summits of the volcanoes Popocatepetl ('Smoking Mountain') and Iztaccihuatl ('The White Lady').

Other important sections of the highlands are the Sierra Madre del Sur, its steep escarpment fronting the Pacific shoreline in southern Mexico, and the mountainous uplands of Oaxaca; both of these fuse to form a highland mass heavily dissected into countless valleys and ranges. Separated from this difficult country by the Isthmus of Tehuantepec, the southeastern highlands form a continuous series of ranges from Chiapas down through Maya territory into lower Central America.

Although snow falls in some places at infrequent intervals, the Mexican highlands are temperate; before denudation by man, they were clothed in pines and oaks, with true boreal forests in the higher ranges. As elsewhere in Mexico, there are two strongly marked seasons – a winter dry period when rain seldom if ever falls, and a summer wet spell. The total rainfall is less than half that of the lowlands, so that occasionally conditions are arid and somewhat precarious for the farmer, in spite of the general richness of the soil. This is especially true of the boundary zone between the agricultural lands and the northern deserts.

The lowlands are confined to relatively narrow strips along the coasts, of which the most important is the plain fronting the Gulf of Mexico. Of alluvial origin, this band of flat land extends unbroken from Louisiana and Texas down through the Mexican states of Tamaulipas, Veracruz, and Tabasco to the Yucatan Peninsula, and played a critical role in the origins of settled life and the growth of civilization in Mexico.

A bridge between the Gulf Coast plain and the narrower and less humid Pacific Coast plain is provided by the Isthmus of Tehuantepec, a constriction in the waist of Mesoamerica, with a gentle topography of low hills and sluggish rivers.

Lowland temperatures are generally torrid throughout the year, except when winter northers come down the Gulf Coast, bringing with them cold rains and drizzle. So heavy is the summer precipitation that in many places the soils are red in color and poor in mineral content as a result of drastic leaching. However, when these

rains cause flooding of rivers, the soils can be highly productive since they are annually replenished with silt along the natural river levees. The winter dry season is generally well marked, so that many of the tropical trees lose their leaves in that season. But where there is an unusually great amount of rain (along with winter northers), one encounters the evergreen canopies and lush growth of the fully developed rain forest. Dotting the lowlands are patches of savannah grassland, sometimes quite extensive, and of little use to the once plowless Mexican farmer.

In response to the opportunities presented by these surroundings, contrasting modes of land cultivation have been developed over the millennia. Highland farmers are quite efficient about their

3 *Chinampas* in the vicinity of Xochimilco, Valley of Mexico.

land, since only a moderate period of fallowing is necessary for the fields. On the other hand, many lowland cultivators, faced with immense forests, the low potential of the soil, weed competition, and winter desiccation, have evolved a shifting form of horticulture which they share with other peoples of the world. This system entails the cutting and burning of the forest from the plot to be sown; a very extensive territory is required for the support of each family since exhausted and weed-infested fields have to be left fallow for as much as ten years. Such a mode of food-getting could never have supported a large population, and we have every evidence to suggest a light occupation of much of the lowland zone throughout its history.

Nonetheless, it is easy to exaggerate the limitations of the lowlands; there are not one but many lowland environments, and a diversity of human responses to them. For instance, one could point to the use of fertile river levees by ancient and modern farmers of the southern Gulf Coast plain, which could have led and *did* lead to increased population density.

Tragically reduced in today's Mexico, game abounded in ancient times. The most important food animals are the white-tailed deer and the collared peccary, found everywhere. Confined to the lowlands are the tapir, the howler monkey, and the spider monkey, all of which are still eaten with relish by the native inhabitants. The lowlands also harbor the jaguar, the largest of the spotted cats and the source of much desired skins for the nobles of civilized Mexico; it must been an object of primitive terror to the early dwellers of the coastal plains. Waterfowl, especially ducks, teem on the lakes and marshes of the uplands, and wild turkeys in the more isolated reaches of the country. Feathers from tropical birds such as the cotinga, the roseate spoonbill, the hummingbird, and above all, the quetzal, with iridescent blue-green plumage, provided rainbow-like splendor for headdresses and other details of costume.

The larger highland lakes, such as Lake Pátzcuaro in Michoacan and the great lake of the Valley of Mexico, teemed with small fish, while the lowland rivers and the coasts provided such an abundance of fish (such as snook and snappers) and turtles that these food resources were more important to ancient peoples than game mammals.

There were no wild species in the New World suitable for domestication as draught animals. The native American horse was exterminated in the Ice Age by man; the South American llama is amenable only as a pack animal; and modern efforts to tame the North American bison have shown that beast to be completely intractable. As a consequence, none of the American Indians prior to their discovery had wheeled vehicles. Ancient Mexico did without any form of overland transportation other than the backs of men, although the principle of the wheel was known and applied to toys and idols of clay. The only warm-blooded animals kept in domestication were the dog and the turkey, the former as well as the latter valuable for its meat. Hives of tiny, stingless bees were exploited for honey by tropical lowlanders.

Climate and man in Mexico

High on the flanks of the hills fringing the Valley of Mexico are clearly visible the remains of beaches left by the great lake – from these alone it would be obvious that conditions in past times were very different from what they are today. A close study of pollen from weather-sensitive plants recovered from deep cores made in the Valley and elsewhere has revealed a long-term fluctuation in rainfall that may well have been a decisive factor in cultural changes on a broad scale.

To understand these fluctuations, we must go back in time more than two million years. Then, for reasons yet unknown, the generally warm and humid climate of the world suffered a profound change, and the Pleistocene, or Ice Age, was initiated. Temperatures dropped and vast quantities of snow were deposited on the ever-rising mountain masses of far northern latitudes, to turn into massive ice sheets which ground their way south over much of northern Eurasia and North America. There were five or more of these glacial advances in the Pleistocene, separated by long inter-glacial periods during which more moderate conditions prevailed. In more southerly regions, such as Mexico, which actually lies within the Tropics, such advances of the northern ice are believed to have been reflected by pluvials, that is, by rainy, cool periods interspersed with dry intervals.

Although geologists do not believe that we have ever really left the Pleistocene, an intense change took place at about 7000 BC, with the final retreat of the ice to the higher latitudes and the beginning of a long interval called the Hypsithermal in which worldwide temperatures were even higher than those of today. The Hypsithermal was broken by only one minor regrowth of the ice sheet in the northern reaches of Canada, the Cochrane Advance of about 5000 BC. From the second millennium before Christ until the present, the world has been in a 'Little Ice Age', with considerable glaciation in far northern climes and a fluctuating but generally greater rainfall than in the Hypsithermal.

These changes must have provided the parameters, the absolute limits, within which each way of life, each type of economy, must have had to operate in ancient Mexico. The period of the Early Hunters was a development of the late Pleistocene, when lush grasslands supported the large grazing animals which they occasionally killed and ate. With the switch to the relatively hot and dry climate of the Hypsithermal, the great herbivores had disappeared, and men had to adapt themselves to a new way of life, the Archaic, under semi-desert conditions in which every sort of plant and animal food was systematically exploited. Men were forced to develop cunning and resourcefulness in the face of starvation. The sudden onset of wetter conditions about 1500 BC, with the prior domestication of food plants, set the stage for the established farming life of the Formative period. Although the height of Mexican civilization was achieved during the Classic period (AD 150–900), the pollen profiles tell us that central Mexico, at least,

4

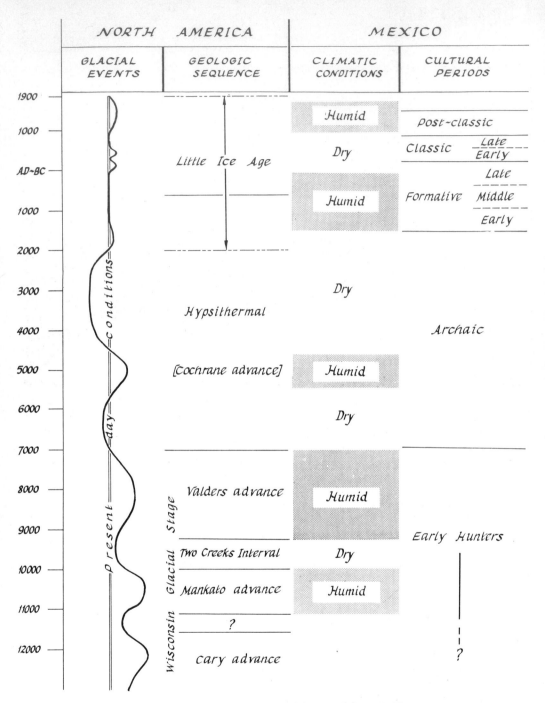

NORTH AMERICA		MEXICO	
GLACIAL EVENTS	GEOLOGIC SEQUENCE	CLIMATIC CONDITIONS	CULTURAL PERIODS

4 Chart of cultural periods and changes of climate in Mexico.

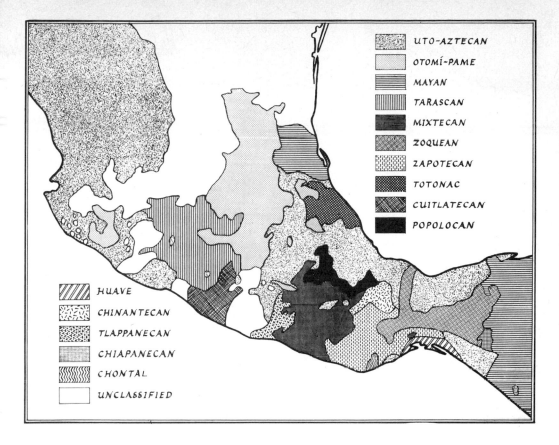

KEY:
UTO-AZTECAN
OTOMÍ-PAME
MAYAN
TARASCAN
MIXTECAN
ZOQUEAN
ZAPOTECAN
TOTONAC
CUITLATECAN
POPOLOCAN

HUAVE
CHINANTECAN
TLAPPANECAN
CHIAPANECAN
CHONTAL
UNCLASSIFIED

became increasingly rainless, and it is more than a possibility that the premature Classic downfall there was due to successive droughts and crop failure. By the later part of the Post-Classic period, marked throughout its course by stepped-up military activities and the growth of conquest states, we have evidence of higher precipitation once more, when the great lake of the Valley of Mexico rose to an almost unprecedented level. The triumphant expansion of the Aztecs, ruling Mexico from their island capital near the western shore of the lake, may in part reflect such favorable conditions.

Full exploration of these suggestions will be left to the chapters that follow.

Languages and peoples

An amazing number of languages were spoken in native Mexico. The situation would be even more confusing if it had not been for the efforts on the part of linguists to group them into families, of which some fourteen have been defined within our area.

5

Of these, the largest and most important to the history of Mexico is Uto-Aztecan, comprising dozens of languages distributed from the northwestern United States as far south as Panama. Since the greatest diversity within this family is found in northwestern Mexico, this wild region has been suggested as the probable

5 Native language groups of Mexico at the time of the Spanish Conquest.

heartland of the Uto-Aztecan peoples. By all odds the major language group within Uto-Aztecan is Nahua, the most significant member of which is Nahuatl, the language of the Aztecs and the *lingua franca* of their empire, still spoken by hundreds of thousands of farmers in the central Mexican highlands and in the state of Guerrero. Since the Conquest, Nahuatl has greatly enriched Mexican Spanish with loan words, and has contributed such words as ocelot, tomato, chocolate, tamale, and copal to the English language.

Tarascan, the tongue of a large kingdom centered on Lake Pátzcuaro in the western part of the Volcanic Cordillera, is totally unrelated to any other language in the world. Otomí-Pame was spoken by peoples who followed a barbarian way of life to the north of the Valley of Mexico, on the fringe of Mesoamerica. Totonac is spoken on the middle Gulf Coast, significantly in the region of the old Tajín civilization. Mixtec and Zapotec are the dominant languages of the state of Oaxaca in southern Mexico, and Zapotec written records go back to at least 400 BC. The Mixe-Zoquean language family is distributed from the Isthmus of Tehuantepec to the Grijalva Depression, and as we shall see in Chapter 5, may have been the language of the ancient Olmecs. Huave was and is spoken by primitive fishermen (now largely turned to cattlemen) on the Pacific coast of the Isthmus. To the east is the large group of Mayan languages; this family has an enigmatic outlier, Huastec, in the area of the Gulf Coast north of the Totonac that is called, naturally enough, the Huasteca. The location of Huastec remains a puzzle for Mesoamericanists. Evidence from the branch of linguistic research known as glottochronology, or lexicostatistics, suggests that it separated from the main group of Mayan languages about 900 BC, but what this means for the development of Mesoamerican cultures has yet to be ascertained.

It would be a fruitless task to try to reconstruct Mexican history merely on the basis of these distributions. Nevertheless, it is evident that the expansion of Uto-Aztecan through much of Mexico must have been drastic; the isolated islands of Nahua speech as far south as lower Central America, Nahua placenames, and the presence of Nahua words in many other languages testify to large-scale movements of peoples. We know in this case of Nahua conquests and migrations having taken place long before the imperialism of the Nahuatl-speaking Aztecs, events recorded in the traditional histories of these peoples. The role that they have played on the stage of New World history has certainly been in the grand style.

Other peoples have probably been more sedentary. But, contradictory as it may seem, while there is fairly good knowledge of the geographic position of most language groups in Mexico at the time of the Conquest, archaeologists are often loth to apply linguistic names to past civilizations unless they are sure beyond any doubt of the identification, as in the case of the Maya, whose writings we have, or the Aztecs. Stones and pottery fragments do not tell us who made them, so that we must be content with the noncommittal names which archaeologists have given us for past peoples.

2
Early Hunters

While the broad outline of what happened during the late Pleistocene in the New World is becoming clearer with every new
discovery of very early artifacts and sites, it is still not established
exactly when man first entered this hemisphere. The *how* is almost
indisputable. The last major stage of the Pleistocene, the Wisconsin
in North America, began around 50,000 years ago and continued,
with many fluctuations, until 9,000 years ago. Because their water
was taken up into ice, the oceans of the world during the advances
of the late Wisconsin were 60 m lower than they stand at present,
sufficiently exposing a platform to form a land bridge at least 1,000
miles wide between Siberia and the western coast of Alaska.
Although an enormous sheet of ice then covered much of North
America as far south as the Great Lakes of today, the land bridge
was ice-free, as was western Alaska and the Yukon valley. The
earliest migrant hunters into America would then have crossed from
Asia through a tundra-covered, treeless, cold region, covered with
thin and patchy snows in winter, and inhabited by small herds of
woolly mammoth, horse, bison, and other ungulates.

All the early skeletons which we have from the Early Hunters   6
stage indicate that these peoples were ancestral American Indians
belonging to the great Mongoloid branch of mankind; no remains of
Peking Man, Neanderthal, or any other archaic form of our genus
have ever been discovered in this hemisphere. Since *Homo sapiens*
arose in the Old World no earlier than the final glacial stage, and
because no indisputably Last Interglacial artifacts have come to
light in North or South America, we may safely assume that man
must have entered Alaska during the Wisconsin. Rising sea levels
beginning at about 8000 BC would have drowned the most feasible
entry route, so that migrations must have predated this. Most
archaeologists would lean to an *early* Wisconsin date for the most
ancient migrations, which probably continued for a considerable
period of time.

Some recent finds tend to back up this 'long chronology' for
man's entry into the hemisphere. At Valsequillo, near Puebla
in southern Mexico, Cynthia Irwin-Williams has found cultural
remains associated with an extinct fauna which included mammoth,
mastodon, horse, antelope, dire wolf, and smaller mammals; the
lack of bifacially worked projectile points suggests a very early date,
confirmed by a radiocarbon determination of about 21,000 years

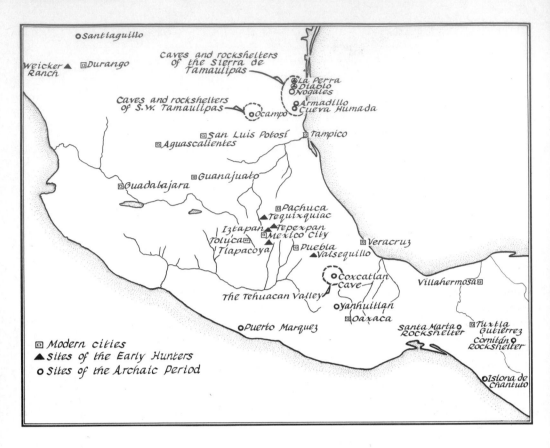

6 Sites of the Early Hunters and Archaic periods.

ago. In the Valley of Mexico itself, dates ranging from 21,000 to 24,000 years ago are possible at the island site of Tlapacoya for a crude industry of choppers, scrapers, flakes, and a blade and burin. Ranging into the earliest known occupation of South America, Dr Richard MacNeish has found in a highland Peruvian cave near Ayacucho an equally crude and very similar industry dated between 16,000 and 21,000 years before the present. The time perspective might be pushed back even further by William Irving's find on the Yukon of fossil bone tools with dates ranging from 26,000 to 29,000 years ago.

The New World must have been an untouched paradise for the first hunting people. Extensive herds of large grazing animals such as mammoths, mastodons, camels, horses, and giant bison roamed through both subcontinents. With ideal conditions such as these, population expansion and spread were probably fairly rapid. Radiocarbon dating has demonstrated that men were hunting sloth, horse, and guanaco at the Straits of Magellan by at least 9000 BC, and there is a reasonable possibility that most of South America was populated long before this.

To understand the significance of finds of late Pleistocene date that have been made in Mexico, it is necessary to consider them in the light of the Early Hunters stage as we now know it for North America as a whole, especially for the United States, where research on this problem has been most intensive. The opinion of many New World archaeologists is that the earliest known remains are those of a very simple culture of hunters and gatherers in which the majority of tools were inconceivably crude, percussion chipped, pebble artifacts. Coarse choppers, chopping tools, scrapers, and knives are found at a number of campsites and open stations in the western United States under conditions of seemingly great antiquity; since this rudimentary inventory is exactly that of the late Pleistocene population of east Asia, it is believed to represent the non-perishable part of the tool-kit of the first immigrants.

By approximately 9500 BC an immense technological change had taken place, with the introduction or invention of fine percussion- and pressure-flaked stone points of the type known as Clovis. These have, extending up from the base on one or both sides, a broad channel or flute formed by the removal of long, narrow flakes by a technique that is not yet well understood. Clovis points are found over much of North America, from Alaska down to Panama; some magnificent specimens come from mammoth 'kill' sites in Arizona near the Mexican border. In the American Southwest, at about 8000 BC, a refinement in fluting produced the well known Folsom point; specimens of this type supersede Clovis, and are often associated with bison 'kills'. All these points, because of their size and weight, are considered to be the 'business end' of darts which were hurled with the aid of a spearthrower (or *atlatl*, to use the Nahuatl term). The bow and arrow was a late arrival in Mexico and was not adopted at all in many areas.

Concurrently with Folsom, which has a somewhat restricted distribution, in the Great Plains as far south as Texas appeared a number of related industries all characterized by bifacially chipped, lanceolate points (Angostura, Scottsbluff, etc.); in actuality, this lanceolate point 'horizon' covers much of Latin America as well. The origin of the techniques and concepts involved in the production of bifacially chipped dart and lance points in this hemisphere is not known, although some have looked to the Old World where very similar industries have existed from a much earlier time level.

Of course, all the above-mentioned tool inventories were the equipment of peoples who were without agriculture and who lived mainly by the chase and the gathering of wild plant foods. From what we know about still extant societies with a similar way of life, such as the Australian aborigines, concentrations of population larger than the small band were quite impossible. Edward Deevey has estimated that on this level of development, corresponding roughly to the Upper Palaeolithic of Europe, 25 square miles of territory are required for the support of one person. In all the New World prior to 7000 BC there may never have been at any one moment in time more than half a million persons, with about 30,000 of these in Mexico – a crude guess, to be sure, but not unreasonable.

Late Pleistocene Mexico presented a landscape considerably

7 Clovis point from the Weicker Ranch, Durango, about 5 cm long.

different from that which we see at the present. Rain poured then on places where it hardly touches today, and many semi-deserts must have been in those remote times a sea of grass. The great lake in the Valley of Mexico, where the most significant finds of the Early Hunters stage have been found, was a great deal broader and deeper, as testified by old strand lines on the surrounding hills.

A single dart point of the Clovis type of quartzite, about 5 cm long, was found on the surface of the Weicker Ranch, some 30 miles west of the city of Durango in northwestern Mexico. Like all Clovis specimens, this is a fluted point fashioned by a combination of percussion- and pressure-flaking and shows the characteristic dulling of the edges at the sides and base (presumably to prevent abrasion of the lashing by which it was bound to the shaft). By analogy with radiocarbon-dated Clovis sites in the United States, this artifact represents an occupation of Mexico as early as the tenth millennium BC.

Freshwater sediments over 75 m thick underlie Mexico City and all areas of the now dry beds of the great lake in the Valley of Mexico. Geological work has established a stratigraphy for the upper part of these deposits that corresponds to the later part of the Pleistocene and all the post-Pleistocene climatic sequence. Crucial to the problem of the ancient occupation in the Valley is the Becerra Formation, divided into an Upper and a Lower. The latter probably pertains to the early or middle Wisconsin Stage, while the Upper Becerra Formation can be assigned with some confidence to the Valders Advance (9000–7000 BC), on the basis of a single radiocarbon date and the kind of artifacts associated with this stratum.

The Upper Becerra is a fine, green muck, and has lenses of ash deposited by the volcanoes that were then in frequent eruption. Over this is a layer of brown, sandy sediments that were deposited at a time when the great lake was shrinking. Presumably this layer represents the first part of the Hypsithermal Interval, broken by the sudden readvance of the Cochrane ice in Canada. A turn to really dry conditions and desiccation of the lake bed is indicated by a layer of *caliche*, or calcium carbonate, marking the climax of the Hypsithermal. From the *caliche* layer to the surface are several layers which probably date from the late Hypsithermal to modern times and which contain abundant potsherds.

As long ago as 1870 the Mexican naturalist Mariano Bárcena discovered the sacrum of an extinct camelid which had been carved to represent the head of an animal, apparently a large member of the dog family, at the locality of Tequixquiac, 42 miles north of Mexico City. This specimen lay at a depth of 12 m below the surface, in deposits of unknown age. One can only indulge in guesswork, but several other lesser finds at Tequixquiac in recent years have been ascribed to the base of the Upper Becerra Formation, and the carved sacrum may well have been found in this layer.

Few finds in recent decades in Mexico have aroused such general interest as the famous 'Tepexpan Man'. In 1949 the geologist Helmut de Terra was engaged in a search for mammoth skeletons

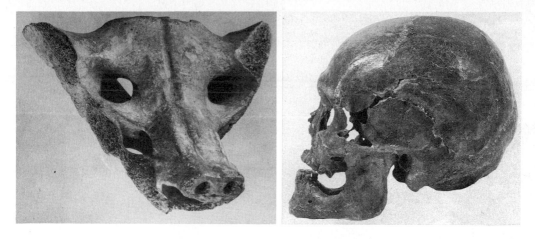

in the vicinity of Tepexpan, on the northeastern edge of the old beds of Lake Texcoco, a locality known to be rich in Pleistocene fossils. Almost as an accidental by-product of his survey, a human skeleton was exposed in one trench. 'Tepexpan Man' appears to have been deliberately buried by his fellows, face down and with the legs drawn up under the body, unaccompanied by any offerings. According to a study by Dr Santiago Genovés, the dead person was a woman of no more than thirty years of age, about 160 cm tall, and not particularly different from Mexican Indians in general. The major problem about 'Tepexpan Man', it should be unequivocally stressed, is the actual stratigraphic position of the skeleton when discovered. According to de Terra, it was found in the Upper Becerra Formation, a stratum known to have fossil elephant remains as well, and underlying the *caliche*. Unfortunately, the inept handling of the excavation makes it unlikely that we shall ever know whether this was so or not. As Marie Wormington has pointed out, the type of burial represented by 'Tepexpan Man' suggests the subsequent Archaic period, when flexed, unaccompanied interments are common, at least in the United States. However, fluorine tests have pretty well demonstrated the contemporaneity of the skeleton with mammalian fossils known to be of Upper Becerra age. 'Tepexpan Man' may be our First Mexican, after all.

Far more satisfactory and less enigmatic results have been obtained on the old lake flats near Santa Isabel Iztapan, only a few miles south of Tepexpan. In 1952, Mexican prehistorians, following up a chance find by workers opening a drainage ditch, excavated the skeleton of an imperial mammoth (*Mammuthus imperator*) which lay entirely within the green muck of the Upper Becerra Formation, and which was therefore Valders in age. The animal had been butchered *in situ*, a fact which could be deduced from the disarticulated position of the bones alone. Most importantly, six human artifacts were indisputably associated with the skeleton. These included a flint projectile point of the type known as Scottsbluff, one of the most widely distributed artifacts of the

8 Animal head carved from the sacrum of an extinct camelid, from Tequixquiac, state of Hidalgo. Early Hunters period.

9 Fossil human skull from Tepexpan, Valley of Mexico. Early Hunters period.

10 The second fossil mammoth from Santa Isabel Iztapan, Valley of Mexico. The hind leg which had become caught in the mud can be seen in the foreground. During butchering, the head and tusks had been dragged back across the body. Early Hunters period.

lanceolate point horizon on the Great Plains of the United States. The other artifacts were utilized in cutting up the mammoth, and comprised a scraper, knife, and fine prismatic blade, all of obsidian, and an endscraper and retouched blade of flint.

10   In 1954, the construction of another ditch by the Santa Isabel Iztapan villagers resulted in the lucky find of a second mammoth 'kill', again with artifacts which had been lost during the butchering process. Here a hind leg of the animal had been caught in the Upper Becerra muck, probably as it was fleeing its human pursuers. During the butchering process, the head and tusks had been dragged back across the body, and some bones showed deep cuts made by stone knives while the meat was being hacked off. Three chipped stone artifacts found among the bones comprise an Angostura point of a dark igneous material, a Lerma point of flint, and a chert, bifacially worked knife. The first two named are of

11   some interest. Angostura points also can be ascribed to the lanceolate-point horizon on the Great Plains, known to be later than the Clovis horizon. Lerma points have an even wider spread in the late Wisconsin Glacial, being found in Texas and northeastern Mexico (where they appear as early as 8000 BC), and are one of the most common types of point ascribed to the Early Hunters stage in South America as far south as Argentina. We have no radiocarbon dates on the Santa Isabel Iztapan finds, but charcoal from a hearth next to a skeleton of still another slaughtered mammoth in the same formation has been dated to 7710 BC ± 400 by this process.

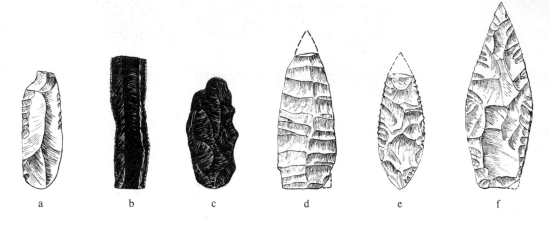

a   b   c   d   e   f

We can reconstruct something of the life and environment of these lacustrine hunters of the Valley of Mexico some 10,000 years ago, although it must be remembered that we lack all knowledge of their campsites and have the chance evidence only of their hunting prowess. The climate was more humid and cooler than that of today; in fact, the now barren outskirts of the Valley were covered with pine forests. In the distance, the young cones of the active volcanoes poured out smoke, ash, and lava, perhaps disturbing the tempo of life in the Valley from time to time, but not seriously disrupting it. The imperial mammoth seems to have favored the swampy margins of the wide, shallow lake. These beasts must have been relatively easy game to organized groups of hunters, who, armed with darts hurled from atlatls and equipped with stone knives and other butchering tools, drove the heavy beasts into shallower water where they became hopelessly mired in the treacherous lake bottom. There each mammoth was isolated and dispatched, although probably not without danger since the risk of impalement by the formidable tusks of the surrounded animal must have been considerable – to kill any elephant with spears would require pluck.

On the northeastern frontier of Mexico, in the state of Tamaulipas, Richard S. MacNeish has revealed in his excavations a long cultural sequence that begins with our primitive Early Hunters. The earliest of these phases, the Diablo Complex, is of some simplicity, comprising only crude, bifacially flaked and uniface tools made from flints or pebbles; choppers, ovoid blades, pebble endscrapers, and crude flake sidescrapers suggest an unspecialized hunting and gathering way of life on the most rudimentary level. Since these artifacts are found in a high terrace of the Canyon Diablo, formed when the river was running very much higher and the climate was obviously much wetter than today, MacNeish has suggested that the Diablo Complex is contemporaneous with the Mankato Advance, 11,000–10,000 B C.

A far better picture of Ice Age life in Mexico comes from the Tehuacan Valley in Puebla, where a large-scale project directed by MacNeish has disclosed a late Pleistocene occupation called the

11 Chipped stone tools found in association with mammoths at Santa Isabel Iztapan. *a*, flint retouched blade; *b*, obsidian prismatic blade; *c*, obsidian knife; *d*, flint Scottsbluff point; *e*, flint Lerma point; *f*, Angostura point. 1/2.

Ajuereado phase. Radiocarbon dates suggest that it ended about 7000 BC, but it must have been in part coeval with the Tepexpan kills. The evidence shows that the climate was cooler and drier than that now prevailing, with open steppe covering the valley floor. In this setting grazed subsequently extinct horse and pronghorn antelope, which were hunted with spears fitted with Lerma points. The inhabitants also sought smaller game, such as jack rabbits, gophers, and rats. The tool technology was totally based upon chipped stone; in addition to projectile points, there were knives, choppers, sidescrapers (for dressing hides), and crude blades. Ground stone tools, which could have been used to prepare vegetable foods, are absent, although some wild plants such as prickly pear cactus and *Setaria* grass were surely harvested by crude means.

12

The inhabitants of Tehuacan during Ajuereado times were probably grouped into about three nomadic families or microbands of four to eight people each, and the evidence of cave-floor occupations shows that camps were changed three or four times a season, since there never was enough food in any one ecological niche to support settled life, a state of affairs which also prevailed throughout the succeeding Archaic stage.

It would be a dangerous misconception to consider this period, viewed as a whole, as merely the time when men hunted huge Pleistocene animals such as mammoth, horse, and so forth. As a matter of fact, in actual habitation sites of this date in Texas and elsewhere in the United States, the vast majority of animal bones come from relatively small animals, as humble as rodents, snakes, snails, and mussels. These people gathered and ate everything that was edible, and probably had to survive some very lean seasons. Since most of the sites which we have are large and conspicuous 'kills', we have been deluded into thinking that we are dealing with some sort of ancient 'big-game hunters' who disdained smaller animals or plant foods. True, large herbivores were slaughtered, but from this we must not assume that the late Pleistocene was a time of plenty. Like the modern Pygmies of the African rain forest, who also hunt elephants, success in the chase probably meant a short feast marked by voracious gluttony, with long intervals of eating whatever they could lay their hands on.

12 Probable community patterns, Ajuereado phase in the Tehuacan Valley. Groups moved from wet-season camps (circles), to fall camps (squares), to dry-season camps (triangles).

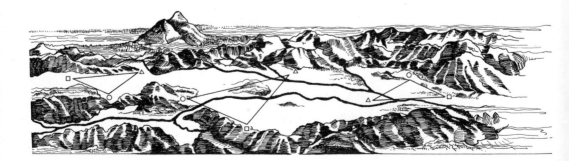

The Archaic period

Six thousand years of almost uninterruptedly high temperatures, as much as 2°C (3.6°F) above present averages in some places, set in on the heels of the Valders ice advance, around 7000 BC. Of course, within this span there were minor fluctuations such as the Cochrane Advance in North America at about 5000 BC, and near 2000 BC the first sporadic indications of a 'Little Ice Age'. The pleasant term 'Climatic Optimum' has been invented for this Hypsithermal period in western Europe, for there the inhabitants of the lands facing on the Atlantic enjoyed significantly wetter as well as warmer weather, perhaps the most balmy ever seen in those regions. Such favorable conditions hardly obtained elsewhere in the world, and in much of North America this long interval was largely one of desiccation. In contrast to the oak forests of humid Europe, vast areas of the New World were transformed into desert wastes.

Odd though it may seem during the Hypsithermal, people continued to live throughout even the most desiccated zones of North America. Species after species of large game perished not long after its onset, or even before it; while climate change has often been advanced as a cause of this ecological disaster, several scholars are convinced that this was a case of 'Pleistocene overkill' by the American Indians themselves. Among the animals which disappeared at this time were the mastodon, mammoth, horse, camel, giant bison, ground sloth, and dire wolf. But the Indians survived. New tools, especially food-grinding implements, new hunting methods, other sources of food, perhaps different forms of shelter, all these enabled people to adapt to radically altered conditions of life.

The new stage of cultural adaptation attained by man in the New World is called the Archaic, and it is the full equivalent of the Mesolithic stage in the western part of the Old World. Denied the rich hunting economy of their late Pleistocene predecessors, small bands of Indians concentrated on more efficient methods of killing smaller game, on fishing and gathering of molluscs, and to an ever-increasing extent on the collection of specific plant foods.

The Desert Culture in North America

In the dry semi-deserts of the Great Basin and southwestern United States, these Archaic hunters and collectors inhabited caves and open sites near the ever-dwindling lakes or by seepages of water. The pattern which enabled men to eke out a livelihood in this inhospitable environment has been named the Desert Culture, which persisted into the nineteenth century among the nomadic Indians of the Great Basin. Its salient features include a sparse population with no groups larger than the band; caves and rockshelters favored for settlements; a subsistence pattern based on the seasonal exploitation of humble food resources such as rabbits, wild plant seeds, and even insects; preparation of plant foods by grinding them on a flat milling stone with a cobble *mano*; abundant basketry, matting, and sandals (known as early as 7000 BC in caves in Oregon); darts tipped with relatively small, percussion-chipped points and hurled by means of the atlatl; a wide variety of scrapers, choppers, scraper planes, and so forth, of remarkably crude manufacture; and the dog, present for the first time in North America early in this development.

It now appears that the Desert Culture pattern is far more widespread in North America than was once thought. Similar Archaic remains are known all the way from Oregon, through the Great Basin and Southwest, including Texas, as far south in Mexico as the Guatemalan border, and now throughout Belize. The region that concerns us here, Mexico, must have been quite hot and dry, as shown by known shrinking of the great lake of the Valley of Mexico and by the overwhelming appearance of dry pollen indicators in the cores at this time.

The discovery in recent decades of an Archaic period of Desert Culture type in Mexico has unexpectedly thrown light on one of the great problems in New World archaeology: where, when, and how were the major food plants domesticated by the American Indian? For it was the cultivation of maize, beans, and squash that made possible all the higher cultures of Mexico, and, to a certain degree, those of Peru as well. In the effort to bridge the gap between the ancient hunting peoples and the first indications of full-blown village life, the researches of Richard S. MacNeish have produced particularly important results, described in this chapter.

The origins of Mexican cultivated plants

There is no simple definition of the term 'domestication'. Quite obviously, there is a difference between the domestication of an animal like the dog or pig, which can and often do revert to the 'wild' state, and a creature, the reproduction of which entirely depends upon the presence of man, such as the Egyptian chicken, which has lost the ability to incubate its own eggs. We are clearly dealing here with a broad spectrum, in which the *degree* of domestication may vary widely; one might thus adopt the definition proposed many years ago by the Russian geneticist Vavilov, and say that it is evolution directed by the interference of man. Basically, this implies that man has in some systematic way tampered with the reproduction of a certain species, a process which may be totally unwitting.

As in animals, in its most extreme form plant domestication ends up with species which cannot reproduce by themselves and which are therefore without wild populations. In the case of cereals and other plants which reproduce by means of seeds, this implies that artificial selection by man has resulted in species which lack the ability to disperse their seeds. Not until that state has been reached can botanists be sure of the presence of domestication in ancient plant remains. It is no accident that all the important food plants of the world belong in this category of totally captive populations, since the reduction of the ability to self-reproduce has resulted in greatly increased food values in the plants concerned.

The importance of maize

The Aztecs believed that their hero-god Quetzalcoatl, who created mankind with his own blood, turned himself into an ant so as to be able to steal a single grain of maize which the ants had hidden inside a mountain; this he gave to men so that they might be nourished. Maize was and is the very basis of settled life in Mexico and, in fact, throughout the regions of the New World civilized in Pre-Columbian times. Speculation as to the origin of this staple has therefore been freely indulged in, with many theories proposed which are no more firmly grounded than the Aztec myth recorded above.

An older generation of archaeologists was raised in the belief that the story of the domestication of maize was completely known. Since maize (*Zea mays*) is a grass with no known wild forms, the search was early started for a closely related species in the wild state. In the highlands of Chiapas and Guatemala, very near the heart of the so-called 'Old Empire' of the Maya, a grass called *teosinte* (*Zea mexicana*) grows in and near Indian cornfields as an unwanted weed; this species is clearly affiliated in some way with maize. It was very early claimed that this was the wild ancestor of maize, and that the process of taming it to meet man's needs was the achievement of the notably advanced Maya. From these people maize was supposed to have spread, along with the arts of civilization, far and wide throughout the New World. The researches of Paul C. Mangelsdorf and his colleagues later suggested that *teosinte* is not the mother of maize, but its daughter, the result of a hybridization between domesticated maize and a truly wild relative, tripsacum (*Zea tripsacum*), an event which must have taken place, if it took place at all, rather late in the history of maize.

The supposed exclusion of *teosinte* from the picture turned the attention of botanists elsewhere. These researches have settled on a strange variety of maize called pod corn, which turns up as a kind of weird sport in primitive cornfields in South America. The kernels of pod corn, unlike those of modern maize, are completely enclosed in glumes, or chaff; furthermore, the ripe ear is only partly covered by husks and therefore may disperse its seeds without the aid of man – a contrast to the 'captive' maize. It was felt that the ancestor of maize must have had many of the characteristics of pod corn, as well as some of the features of pop corn which is primitive in having small, hard seeds (this is the reason why it has to be popped). Experiments in crossing modern pod corn with pop corn revealed the true nature of the hereditary factors involved in the domestication of maize, as well as some of the more probable features which this hypothetical ancestor must have possessed. The wild progenitor was apparently a small plant with a single stalk and a single influorescence at the top – that is, a female flower (ear) which bore the seeds after fertilization, and a male flower (tassel) at the top. The plant would have been self-fertilizing, of course, and like pod corn today had heavy chaff covering the kernels, but greatly reduced husks.

Apparently a single mutation was responsible for many changes in the plant, a genetic alteration which resulted in multiple effects. The primary change was a reduction in glumes or chaff, releasing energy for the production of a larger cob with more and larger kernels. This mutation also lowered the position of the inflorescences, or flowers, and it is known that the lower the ear, the stronger the stalk, with a greater capacity for producing larger ears; the more likely it is to develop only female flowers which produce kernels when pollinated (the male tassel remains at the top of the plant); and the longer the shanks attaching the ear to the stalk – shanks which give rise to more husks surrounding the ear. The end result of this mutation is a plant which is not adapted to wild conditions.

Here is where man would have stepped in. A group of primitive collectors of plant food might have favored wild maize plants which exhibited the larger ears and brought the harvest back to their camps, some of the seeds eventually ending up in the messy refuse heaps which accompany this sort of life. Thus, the mutants would have been captured by man and artificially selected by him – a form of conscious and unconscious domestication together. Once these Indians learned that the plants would be more productive if the plots were cleared of weeds, new avenues in the improvement of maize were opened. One might logically ask, but why did wild maize become extinct? Mangelsdorf believes that domesticated maize backcrossed with wild populations so frequently in early history that the latter were eliminated by taking on the mutant gene resulting in non-dispersal of seeds. In like manner, continued backcrossing between *teosinte* and maize in modern Indian fields is bringing these two kinds of *Zea* increasingly close to one another.

Where did these events take place? Botanists have fluctuated in their search from Mesoamerica to South America, and some have leaned to multiple points of origin in the New World. Preposterous claims of maize origins in Asia, Africa, or the Near East may be dismissed. Fossil evidence casting light on this problem comes from a core made in the Valley of Mexico. At a depth of 61 m, in deposits which must be at least 80,000 years old and which therefore certainly predate man's presence there, were found pollen grains which demonstrate conclusively that wild maize was in Mexico by this date. To the north of Mesoamerica proper, in a rockshelter called Bat Cave in south central New Mexico, charred cobs of an exceptionally primitive kind of maize have been found along with pre-pottery remains of Desert Culture aspect, all dating to about 2500 BC. The plant was apparently domesticated, but the cobs are no larger than a strawberry; it seems that these represent a very early stage in the domestication process. Thus, North rather than South America, and more specifically the region in and near Mexico, would seem to hold the answer which has been sought for so long. It is this likelihood which has made more recent work in Mexico so interesting.

The *teosinte* controversy, however, has recently returned to haunt us once more. The absence of a living wild ancestor for maize continued to preoccupy the geneticist George Beadle, and he and other botanists have again proposed *teosinte* as the progenitor. As can well be imagined, feelings run high on this issue. Archaeology has not yet fully resolved the argument, but it is. likely that Mangelsdorf is right. A recent discovery in the state of Jalisco, announced in 1979, may provide the solution. This is a hitherto unknown species of perennial *teosinte* (*Zea diploperennis*) which has the same chromosome number as maize and freely crosses with it. Experiments have now shown that the annual *teosintes* are *not* the hybrid offspring of maize and *Tripsacum*, but rather of this perennial *teosinte* and what was probably a very early form of domestic maize; and that other results of this hybridization might have been new pod corn varieties amenable to improvement under man's tutelage. Annual *teosinte* is still believed to have played a major role in the subsequent development of maize through backcrossing with it.

Other cultigens

While maize is at the center of the Mesoamerican food complex, other vegetable foods always accompany it. The pre-Spanish Mexicans consumed an extraordinary array of plant foods, from various kinds of beans to squashes to chili peppers to fruits. In fact, it is difficult to imagine what the world's cuisines were like before the discovery of Mexico and Peru. The list in the accompanying table (p. 34) is incomplete, and does not, of course, give all the varieties or races of each plant.

The common bean, known in many varieties today, is the most popular in Mexican diets and presumably has been so since very early periods. Its nutritional importance stems from the fact that its proteins complement those of maize. On the basis of a distribution of wild forms, Vavilov suggested a primary domestication in Mexico or Guatemala.

Of squashes, there are three major species in Mexico: pumpkin, warty or crookneck squash, and walnut squash, the forms of all of which are virtually legion, as any visitor to a Mexican food market can readily testify. The origins of all of these from wild ancestors or through hybridization are very little understood, although the sequence of their appearance in Mexico is now established. The same might be said of chili peppers, now the major ingredient in 'hot' foods the world over, but of Mexican and Peruvian origin; the

The domestic plants of pre-Spanish Mexico

COMMON NAME	LATIN NAME	COMMENTS
*Avocado	*Persea americana*	
Amaranth	*Amaranthus hybridus*	Pot herb, grain
*Annatto	*Bixa orellana*	Flavoring, food coloring
Black nightshade	*Solanum nigrum*	Pot herb
Black sapote	*Diospyros ebenaster*	Fruit tree
Bottle gourd	*Lagenaria siceraria*	Container
*Cacao	*Theobroma cacao*	Beans, the source of chocolate, used for money
*Calabash tree	*Crescentia cujete*	Rind of fruit used as container
*Cashew	*Anacardium occidentale*	Fruit tree
Century plant	*Agave americana*	Source of pulque wine, leaves eaten and used for fiber
Chayote	*Sechium edule*	Squash-like fruit
Chía	*Salvia hispanica*	Seeds used for beverage, oil
Chili pepper	*Capsicum frutescens, C. annuum*	
Common bean	*Phaseolus vulgaris*	
Copal	*Protium copal*	Resin used as incense
Cotton	*Gossypium hirsutum*	
Goosefoot	*Chenopodium* spp.	Pot herb
*Guava	*Psidium guajava*	Fruit tree
*Hog plum	*Spondias mombin*	Fruit tree
Husk tomato or tomatillo	*Physalis ixocarpa*	Vegetable
Indigo	*Indigofera suffruticosa*	Dye
Jack bean	*Canavalia ensiformis*	
Maize	*Zea mays*	
*Manioc	*Manihot esculenta*	Root crop
*Papaya	*Carica papaya*	Fruit tree
Peanut	*Arachis hypogaea*	Of Andean origin
*Pitahaya	*Hylocereus undatus*	Fruit of epiphytic cactus
Prickly pear	*Opuntia* spp.	Fruit and cactus pods eaten
Pumpkin	*Cucurbita pepo*	
*Rubber	*Castilla elastica*	Trunk tapped for latex
*Sapota	*Pouteria mammosa*	Fruit tree
Scarlet runner bean	*Phaseolus coccineus*	
*Soursop	*Annona muricata*	Fruit tree
*Star-apple	*Chrysophyllum cainito*	Fruit tree
Sweet potato	*Ipomoea batatas*	
Tepary bean	*Phaseolus acutifolius*	
Tobacco	*Nicotiana tabacum*	
Tomato	*Lycopersicon esculentum*	
*Vanilla	*Vanilla planifolia*	An epiphytic orchid
Walnut squash	*Cucurbita mixta*	
Warty (crookneck) squash	*Cucurbita moschata*	
White sapota	*Casimiroa edulis*	Fruit tree
*Yam bean	*Pachyrrhizos erosus*	Has edible tuber
Yucca	*Yucca elephantipes*	Hedges; flowers edible

*grown mainly in the lowlands

major problem with this seasoning (also an important source of vitamins to Indian populations) is the difficulty of distinguishing between wild and domesticated seeds.

Archaeological evidence for the origin of many other cultigens is rare to non-existent, in part due to the perishable nature of root crops. Thus, the antiquity and role of manioc in the tropical lowlands of Mesoamerica are not known, in spite of the fact that this is an important food plant there today. I have also not mentioned the decorative plants of Mexico, such as the dahlia, marigold, and zinnia; the marigold, for instance, has a significant part to play in the long roster of Mexican medicinal plants. Also omitted are economically important trees which are protected rather than actually domesticated, such as the breadnut tree, the sacred ceiba (symbolic of the Tree of Life), mahogany, and the sapodilla tree, which produced valuable fruit, wood, and chicle latex for chewing gum.

Caves and rockshelters of northeastern Mexico

Richard MacNeish's search for the origins of agriculture and settled life in Mexico first led him to the almost rainless, semi-desert environment of Tamaulipas, the northeasternmost Mexican state. It is actually beyond the frontier of Mesoamerica: the tribes encountered by the Spaniards in this backward region were, with few exceptions, hunters and collectors without knowledge of cultivation. MacNeish was drawn to this region because the aridity of Tamaulipas has meant ideal conditions of preservation in cave and rockshelter sites, of which a good many were discovered. In the course of his excavations, he uncovered the first evidence for an entirely new stage in the prehistory of Mexico: the Archaic or 'incipient agricultural' period, lasting from about 6500 BC to after 2000 BC.

The Archaic Tamaulipas tool inventory is fairly typical of the Desert Culture throughout western and southern North America. In chipped stone, there were scrapers, choppers, pebble hammer-stones, and disk scrapers, most of which were probably used in the preparation of vegetable foods; projectile points, used in the hunting of deer, were fixed to dart shafts with resin. Plant products were also processed with ground stone tools, such as mortars, pestles, manos, and crude milling stones. MacNeish concludes that the economy largely rested upon hunting, collecting, and the grinding of wild seeds. As part of this complex, there were simple nets and turned and coiled baskets, while cordage was made from

13

13 Characteristic stone tools of the Archaic in Tamaulipas. *a*, mortar; *b*, hand stone or mano; *c*, milling stone. 1/4.

14 the fiber of wild plants like yucca and agave. People slept on twilled mats; these, known as *petates*, are still standard sleeping gear for millions of Indians in back-country Mexico.

Plant materials and dried feces, or coprolites, were remarkably well preserved and abundant, for the ancient inhabitants of these rockshelters had only scanty notions of hygiene. The diet was heavy in vegetable foods, some of which came from domesticated plants. Earliest of all is the bottle gourd; this appeared by about 6500 BC. It is even older in the Archaic period of Oaxaca and is thus the most ancient cultigen of the New World. The history of the bottle gourd, usable only as a container since the meat is inedible, is puzzling. It is believed by botanists to be of Old World origin, probably with an initial center of domestication in Africa. Tests have shown that the seeds are viable after the dried gourd has been immersed for several years in sea water. Accordingly, the likelihood is that the plant floated from Africa to the New World to land on some eastern shore. How, then, did the American Indian adopt it as his own? It is remotely possible that some beachcomber of a distant era came across the gourd by accident, carried it back to his camp and sowed the seeds. One hardly needs to stress that this reconstruction is pure fantasy, but I am not prepared to adopt the alternative explanation, namely that African voyagers carried the gourd with them on a sea trip to the west at this early date.

Other plants occur in the Tamaulipas sequence at somewhat later dates, including pumpkin, scarlet runner beans, chili peppers, common beans, and squashes, in that order. There was no wild maize in MacNeish's excavations, but the cobs of a tiny-eared pop corn with many pod corn characteristics appears between 3000 and 2200 BC. This suggested to MacNeish that he should be looking further south for the origins of maize.

14 Ovoid biface of obsidian and matting fragment, Archaic period of Tamaulipas. 1/2.

Santa Marta rockshelter

As one travels west from the Grijalva Basin, the Chiapas highlands grow increasingly arid. Santa Marta rockshelter lies in this dry zone, near the town of Ocozocoautla on the Pan American Highway, and was tested by MacNeish and Fredrick Peterson in 1959. Five successive Archaic occupations in the cave were directly overlain by pottery-bearing deposits ascribable to the Early Formative horizon. Radiocarbon dates for the Archaic levels indicate a span from at least 6700 BC through an extremely dry post-Cochrane period (after 5000 BC). The complex of tool and point types duplicates that of Tamaulipas, and includes dart points, gouges, scraper planes, pebble manos and boulder querns, etc. Four burials were found together, three of them flexed in fetal posture and one extended above, all the dead having been covered as a group with metates. Burials of this sort occur in Desert Culture contexts as far north as Wyoming.

Maize pollen makes its appearance only in the Early Formative occupation, both pollens and other maize plant parts being completely absent from the pre-pottery levels. So, we might draw the conclusion that in the search for maize origins, Chiapas, on the southeastern periphery of Mexico, is perhaps too far south, just as Tamaulipas appears to be too much to the north.

The Tehuacan Valley

The most exciting discovery in Mexican archaeology in recent decades has been of actual remains of wild maize, found in archaeological deposits in highland Mexico. In 1960, MacNeish turned his attention to the Tehuacan Valley in southeastern Puebla, some 130 miles southeast of Mexico City. Lying in the rain shadow

15 View of the Tehuacan Valley, looking out from Coxcatlan Cave.

15 of the Sierra Madre range which protects it on the east, the Valley is an arid cactus- and thorn-scrub-covered desert not unlike southern Arizona. So dry is it that effective agriculture capable of supporting a large population is only possible with irrigation, a technique that goes back here to the first millennium BC. MacNeish's preliminary reconnaissance of the bone-dry caves and rockshelters which border the Valley led to a four-season project which uncovered, at long last, cobs of wild maize as well as of the earliest cultivated variety.

It will be remembered that the Ajuereado phase, an Early Hunters occupation of the Valley, ended about 7000 BC. During the succeeding El Riego phase (c. 7000–5000 BC), two significant changes had come about. The first is that the climate turned warmer, perhaps resulting (with human help) in the disappearance of 'big game'. The second is that by the end of the phase, the Tehuacan people had begun interfering with the evolution of certain plants: surely domesticated were the avocado, chili peppers, amaranth (this remained a grain of secondary importance in the highlands right through the Spanish Conquest), and walnut squash. As in Tamaulipas, the preponderance of vegetable food, both wild and domesticated, in the diet is reflected by numerous mortars and pestles, and by milling stones and pebble manos; large plano-convex scrapers and choppers were probably used for pulping various plant materials. Chipped projectile points for atlatl-propelled darts are present, used in hunting deer and other relatively small game.

There are some surprising features in El Riego. Two bolls of domestic cotton were recovered, apparently the world's first. Some quite elaborate burials from the phase were found in caves, the bodies being wrapped in blankets and nets, and the heads sometimes removed, ceremonially smashed, and deposited in baskets; in a burial group of two children, the head of the older was found in a basket resting on the chest of the younger. Possibly we are confronted here with a very early case of human sacrifice.

While population size had increased, the El Riego people remained seasonally nomadic. During the dry season, camps were occupied by microbands which lived mainly by hunting. In the spring, these moved into the slopes of the Valley, collecting seeds, and in the summer 'wet season' they were able to pick fruit. Perhaps when there was more rain than usual, they were able to coalesce into macrobands. In the fall, with a diminution of food supplies, they moved back to their winter abodes.

One of the great transition points in New World prehistory is to be seen in the Coxcatlan phase (c. 5000–3400 BC). The economy and settlement pattern remained much the same, but to the list of domesticates were added the bottle gourd, common bean, black sapote, and warty squash – the evidence is now quite clear that these and other plants were domesticated in different places and at different times. Most important is the appearance of maize for the first time anywhere in the New World. This proved to be of two types, a wild variety and an early domesticated one which was

16 Cob of wild maize from the Coxcatlan phase, Tehuacan Valley.

probably planted, like already existing cultigens, when microbands came together in the spring. The minuscule cobs of wild maize so 16 closely approach the reconstructed ancestor of maize in every respect, that Mangelsdorf is confident that the ancestor of corn has been found. In particular, they exhibit the extended glumes, the tiny kernel size, and the bearing of the male tassel on the female ear of the hypothetical progenitor, as well as showing no variation among themselves, a wild characteristic. However, as recent proponents of the *teosinte* theory of maize origins have pointed out, they also look distressingly like *teosinte*!

The revived dispute has been largely settled. The Tehuacan cobs are those of pod corn, and archaeological and botanic evidence shows that annual *teosinte* never could have been their progenitor. On the other hand, perennial *teosinte* must have crossed at a very early date with pod corn to produce annual *teosinte* and perhaps the ancestral forms of domestic maize. The controversy, nevertheless, may be of more interest to plant geneticists than to students of ancient Mexican culture, for the important point to remember is that the world's most productive domesticated plant had now come under human control; the process of domestication, in MacNeish's present way of thinking, took place somewhere in the Puebla-Oaxaca region during the 7000 to 5000 BC time period.

The succeeding Abejas phase (*c.* 3400–2300 BC) saw a distinct change in the Tehuacan settlement pattern, with small hamlets of five to ten pithouses down on the Valley floor. Domestic plants newly added to the cuisine were tepary beans, perhaps the pumpkin, and hybrid maize showing introgression ('capture' of genes by backcrossing) with *teosinte*. While a study by the late Eric Callen of Abejas coprolites reveals that seventy percent of the diet was still based on wild plants and animals, the increasing cultivation of crops for storage in specially made caches and pits was associated with longer and longer stays in band encampments. The result was the possibility of staying in one place all year; sedentism was gradually replacing nomadism.

It will be seen in the next chapter that Early Formative pottery centers on the neckless jar or *tecomate*, and the flat-bottomed bowl with outslanting sides. It is probably significant that in Abejas these same shapes are seen in beautifully made-ground stone vessels, perhaps prototypes for later ceramics.

In fact, during the final Archaic phase in the Valley, the poorly known Purrón (c. 2300–1500 BC), crude, gravel-tempered pottery makes its appearance, in some of the same shapes that are seen in the Abejas stone vessels. The so-called 'Pox pottery', found by Charles and Ellen Brush in middens on the coast of Guerrero, is close in appearance to the Purrón ceramics and has similarly early radiocarbon dates. Nonetheless, it is quite unlikely that pottery – that index fossil of fully sedentary life – was independently developed in Mesoamerica, for agricultural villages with well-developed ceramics have a far greater antiquity along the Caribbean and Pacific coasts of northern South America, and many archaeologists believe that the idea of firing clay to make vessels spread from there to Mexico.

Other Archaic sites

Until recently, almost all the significant information on the Mexican Archaic had come from Tamaulipas and Tehuacan, but new excavations have appreciably added to the total picture. In the Valley of Oaxaca, Kent Flannery and his associates have uncovered a long preceramic sequence paralleling that of Tehuacan in some respects, but adding new and sometimes contradictory data. Most of Flannery's sites are caves, as in Tehuacan, but the open-air site of Geo-Shih was particularly interesting as it showed evidence of activity features, such as a possible dance-floor area bordered with stones. As for domesticates, there are pollen grains of the genus *Zea* in 7400–6700 BC levels, which palaeobotanist James Schoenwetter says are in the size range of *teosinte*, thus adding to the controversy. Rinds of bottle gourds and seeds and peduncles of pumpkins are also this early, and so predate their appearance in Tehuacan.

The role of the lowlands, plagued by poor archaeological preservation, is relatively unknown. There can be no question that maize is a seed crop of highland origin, but lowland root crops like manioc leave little if any archaeological evidence. Thus, while there are good data on hunting, gathering, and fishing for an extensive Archaic village found by Jeffrey Wilkerson at Santa Luisa, on the coast of northern Veracruz, the absence of manos and metates need not necessarily mean an absence of cultivation, since manioc preparation does not require these. Similarly, pre-pottery levels in shell middens at Puerto Marquez and Islona de Chantuto on the Pacific coast may well be manifestations of an otherwise unknown 'incipient agricultural' way of life.

One of the most important Archaic discoveries has been at Tlapacoya, once an isolated island in the southern part of the Valley of Mexico; circular houses like those of the Abejas phase have been uncovered, along with an extremely crude female figurine of pottery, dated 2300 BC ± 100, the oldest discovered in Mesoamerica and apparently the beginning of a tradition that was to flourish in the Formative.

The Archaic period and the origins of settled life

The idea that the invention and adoption of food production led to a 'revolution' in the advancement of mankind was elaborated by the late V. Gordon Childe and has influenced the way of thinking of almost all who deal with this point in man's history. At the time that he wrote (1925–56), almost nothing was known of the transition between the hunting and gathering and the food-producing way of life, either in the Old World or in the New. The mere absence of the evidence made the jump seem almost more sudden than recent work has shown it actually to have been. Now, for both Peru and Mexico, we have evidence of a very slow progress towards fully settled life: the alleged 'revolution' was seemingly more in the nature of a leisurely evolution. Yet, it cannot be denied that the consequences of food production were in the long run of the greatest importance. Deevey has demonstrated that the density of population of peoples on the Neolithic (or Formative) level of food-getting is 25 times greater than the figure for primitive hunters and gatherers – the domestication of plants and animals obviously resulted in a quantum increase in the world's population, no matter how long the process took.

In Mexico, and probably in Mesoamerica in general, the development of plant cultivation took place during the Archaic period in a context which is almost indistinguishable from that of the Desert Culture, known so well in the Great Basin country of the American West. Back in this remote time, the ancestors of the mighty Aztecs and other civilized peoples of Mexico probably closely resembled the miserable 'Digger Indians' of Nevada and California, so despised by Mark Twain and other western travellers of the Victorian era. Semi-nomadic bands were forced into a seasonal cycle of hunting and collecting by the poverty of the rainless Mexican environment. As the Hypsithermal wore on, however, their efficiency at collecting plant foods began to outweigh their hunting prowess, with an increasing amount of settling down – seasonal camps took on the appearance of tiny villages. As the result of systematic exploitation of certain kinds of plants, especially of wild grasses like maize, vegetable foods and their energy were tamed and captured. According to present evidence, the process began with the bottle gourd, which may have been an accidental introduction, followed by pumpkins, beans, and chili peppers. Maize was most likely domesticated in southern Mexico by the middle of the sixth millennium before Christ, although at that time it hardly resembled the giant hybrid plants of modern Iowa cornfields. Other domesticated food plants are much later and a few, like the peanut, were probably disseminated to Mexico from South America in post-Archaic times.

By the time of the first village-farming cultures, at the onset of the Formative, there were already present many of the features of settled life: all the important domesticates, the milling stones and manos on which maize was prepared, baskets, nets, cordage, mats, and apparently even wattle-and-daub houses. With the elaboration of pottery, almost certainly introduced from the lowland regions of South America, and with the yet mysterious improvement of maize at this great transition, the stage is set for a way of life that has remained unaltered to this day in the peaceful backwaters of Mexico.

17 Sites of the Formative period. The inset shows the distribution of Formative centers in the Valley of Mexico.

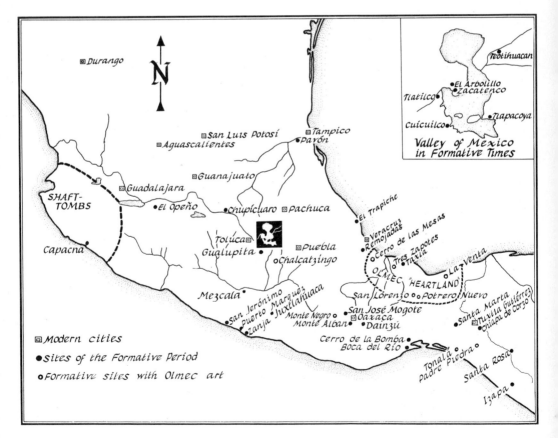

4
The Formative period:
early villagers

In the late nineteenth century, there was really no idea at all of the sequence of development in pre-Spanish Mexico. Of course, everyone knew perfectly well that the Aztecs were quite late, and there was a vague feeling that the great ruins of Teotihuacan were somehow the products of an earlier people, but that was about all. Imagine the delight, then, of Mexican antiquarians when there began to appear in their collections little, handmade, clay figurines, of a naïve and amusing style totally removed from that of the mold-made products of later peoples in the Valley of Mexico. Most astonishing was their obvious antiquity, for some had been recovered from deposits underlying the *Pedregal*, the lava covering much of the southwestern part of the Valley. Scholars, prone to labels, immediately named the culture which had produced the figurines and the very abundant pottery associated with it 'Archaic', and in 1911 and 1912 Manuel Gamio demonstrated stratigraphically that the central Mexican sequence runs from earliest to latest: 'Archaic', Teotihuacan, Aztec.

It was not very long before the 'Archaic' or something like it was turning up all over Mexico and Central America, wherever, in fact, the archaeological spade went deep enough. Similar materials were found even in South America: in Peru, along the waterways of the Amazon basin, and on the Caribbean coast of Venezuela. On the basis of this distribution, Herbert J. Spinden in 1917 proposed that there was an 'Archaic' basement, so to speak, underlying all the civilizations of the Western Hemisphere, a unitary culture which had originated with the supposed first domestication of maize in the Valley of Mexico and which had spread with that plant everywhere, bearing along the little figurines as a hallmark. Quite naturally, this idea, which was based on incomplete and faulty evidence, met with very determined opposition, especially by those whose subsequent delvings into 'Archaic' remains had shown them the considerable diversity within this allegedly monolithic culture.

Let us define the Formative as that epoch when farming based on 17 maize, beans, and squash really became effective – effective in the sense that villages, and hamlets had sprung up everywhere in Mexico. As such, the Formative period is quite comparable to the

Neolithic of the Old World, and almost all the Neolithic arts, with the exception of animal husbandry, were present: the construction of compact settlements, pottery, loom weaving, working of stone by grinding as well as chipping, and the modeling of female figurines in clay.

Villages mean more people, and more people are, broadly speaking, the result of a greatly increased supply of food. What had happened to bring this about? As outlined in the previous chapter, the plants involved had already been domesticated for several millennia prior to the Formative. We may be seeing the result of a hasty improvement in the size and number of kernels of the maize ear through increased introgression of *teosinte*. A resulting population spiral of the most Malthusian sort could have suddenly filled all of Mexico with land-hungry farmers, and camps and hamlets might have become permanently settled villages in almost a few generations.

When did this take place? Somewhat arbitrarily, it must be admitted, we set the lower limits of the Formative at the first appearance of pottery in abundance, about 1500 BC according to recent radiocarbon dates. The upper boundary is more problematical. In the lowland Maya area, the first carved monuments appear *c.* AD 300, and this is usually taken as the beginning of the Classic throughout Mesoamerica. However, in central Mexico, the Classic is initiated *c.* AD 150, when the great city of Teotihuacan takes its present shape; we shall thus adopt the latter date as the termination of the Formative. These dates therefore span some sixteen and a half centuries.

It might also be reasonably asked why it took so long for the Mexicans to cross the threshold to village-farming life. In the Old World this event first occurred, along the hilly flanks of Mesopotamia, as early as the seventh millennium before Christ, not very much later than the first experimentation with plant and animal domestication. In Mexico, where the American Indian originally took this step, the process of domestication took at least four and a half millennia; was this delay caused by the lack of domesticable animals, by the nature of the plants domesticated, by the cultural milieu of Mexico, or by some other factor? We do not yet know the answer, but a handicap of this kind is the real reason why sixteenth-century Mexico was the inferior of Europe, for once past the frontier into peasant life, ancient Mexican culture unfolded at the same rate as did that of the Old World. Given this late start, the civilization that Cortés destroyed should be compared not to Renaissance Europe, but to the Bronze Age of the Near East and China.

Archaeologists are generally agreed that the Formative development can be divided into three parts: Early, from 1500 to 900 BC; Middle, from 900 to 300 BC; and Late, from 300 BC to AD 150. It is also increasingly apparent, as we shall see, that both simple village cultures and advanced states can be detected in all three subperiods. The emerging picture is far more intricate than could have been imagined fifty or even twenty years ago.

The Early Formative in Chiapas

Knowledge of the Early Formative is relatively recent; it began in the 1950s with the interest of the New World Archaeological Foundation in Chiapa de Corzo. Excavations in that site, lying in the center of the Grijalva Depression of Chiapas, have disclosed no less than eighteen successive occupations from the earliest times to the present. For much of its history, the Grijalva drainage basin seems to have been little more than a buffer state between the Maya to the east and an assortment of lesser nations to the west, south, and north. However, in the Formative period each of several distinctive cultures was linked to other more distant village and state cultures of southeastern Mexico.

As reconstructed from debris recovered deep in a test pit, the Chiapa I, or Cotorra, phase presents us with the very beginnings of Formative life. A single radiocarbon date falls in the thirteenth century BC, but the total span of the culture is estimated to be about

18

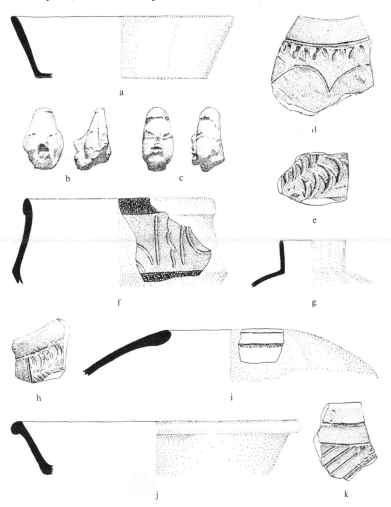

18 Early Formative ceramics, Chiapa I phase (1500–1000 BC), from Chiapa de Corzo. *a*, dish; *b–c*, figurine heads; *d, e, h, i, k*, rim fragments from neckless jars (*e* and *h* are rocker-stamped); *g*, fragment of necked jar; *j*, dish with thickened rim. *a f, h, j* and *k*, 3/8; *g* and *i*, 3/16.

1500 to 1000 BC. Admittedly we have only a fragmentary picture of the first farmers at Chiapa de Corzo, but they prepared their maize on simple milling stones which are heavily worn and thus must have been rare, and they manufactured solid, handmade clay figurines. Their pottery was advanced in technique and quite sophisticated in form and decoration. Most of it consists of a hard, monochrome white or two-color red-and-white ware, in the shape of dishes and large storage jars which might be either simple globular or else necked. Of some interest is the plastic decoration found on the rims of otherwise plain neckless jars: brushing with a handful of vegetable fibers, rows of gouges effected with the thumbnail, dimples popped out from the vessel interior, and plain rocker-stamping.

Now, rocker-stamping is a most peculiar way to alter the surface of a jar or dish. The trick is to 'walk' the edge of a crescentic implement held in the hand across the damp clay in such a way that curved, zigzag patterns are produced. Rocker-stamping is found on pots of the allied and coeval Ocós culture of the Pacific coast of Guatemala, where the tool used was the crinkly edge of a cardium shell; and, in fact, the technique was known to Formative peoples all the way from the Valley of Mexico to Peru. Whatever its point of origin, rocker-stamping is thought to have spread through the advanced regions of the New World at a fairly early date.

Vestiges of a culture much like Chiapa I lie just above the latest Archaic occupation of Santa Marta cave, further west in Chiapas (see Chapter 3), and are accompanied by the pollen of maize and other plants indicating a very wet phase. Quite certainly, the farmers of the Early Formative enjoyed a climate which contrasted with the rainless conditions of the preceding Archaic.

Early Formative villagers in Oaxaca

The Valley of Oaxaca, the homeland of the Zapotec people and the locus of the remarkable Monte Albán culture of later periods, is three-armed and shaped like an inverted Y. It was once thought that prior to the Monte Albán I phase (c. 500–200 BC), the Valley was completely filled with a lake, and that therefore no earlier cultural remains would ever be found. This has been totally disproved by the large-scale University of Michigan archaeological-ecological project, directed by Kent V. Flannery, which has shown that there was always a river valley here, and never a lake. Furthermore, the Flannery group has uncovered a cultural sequence extending all the way from the earliest preceramic Archaic, right up through Monte Albán I.

The impressive strides which anthropology and ecology have made during the last two decades in the understanding of the prehistoric past can be seen in the Michigan excavations at San José Mogote, an important Formative center 6¼ miles north-northwest of Monte Albán in the Etla arm of the Valley. During the San José phase (1150–850 BC), this was a village of 80 to 120 households covering about 20 hectares, with an estimated population of 400 to

600 persons. Carbonized seeds recovered by the flotation method show that a number of crops were raised, probably on the high alluvium: maize, chili peppers, squashes, and possibly the avocado (although this may have been traded in from the lowlands). Our old friend *teosinte* grew in cornfields and crossed with local maize, either by accident or design.

Food storage was probably the main function of the bell-shaped pits which here, as elsewhere in Formative Mesoamerica, are associated with household clusters. Many could have held a metric ton of maize, and if capped with a flat rock, might have inhibited insect growth through lack of oxygen. As they 'soured' or otherwise lost their usefulness for preservation of grain, they were employed for other purposes, such as the preservation of household items and implements, or for refuse disposal, or even as burial places.

The only domestic animals eaten were dogs – the principal source of meat for much of Formative Mesoamerica – and turkeys – understandably rare because that familiar bird consumes very large quantities of corn and is thus expensive to raise. Wild animals in the San José Mogote diet were cottontail rabbits; and deer and peccary which were hunted on the mountain slopes, an area which also produced acorns and black walnuts.

Houses were rectangular and about 6 m long, with slightly sunken floors of clay covered with river sand. The sides were of vertical canes between wooden posts, and were daubed with mud, then white-washed; roofs were thatched. Sleeping arrangements were typically Mesoamerican: people slept on mats rolled out on the floor. The Michigan project found that there was a division of labor between and within households. Some houses, for instance, specialized in the manufacture of small, flat mirrors made of magnetite, an iron ore which takes a high polish. Within houses, clear signs of an area mainly used by women were concentrations of bone needles, deer bone cornhuskers, and spindle whorls made from potsherds. Men's place in households was indicated by chipped stone debris and by stone burins and drills used in the manufacture of shell and mica ornaments.

Not all households were alike in status, either, and the concentration of magnetite mirrors – an item rich in symbolic prestige since it was connected, as we shall see, with the burgeoning and contemporary Olmec civilization of the Gulf Coast – was unequal across the village. Furthermore, there was a marked degree of social differentiation in the goods accompanying burials: high-status individuals tended to have burial offerings like mirrors, cut shell, jade labrets and earspools, and above all gray or white pottery vessels with Olmec designs. This was no egalitarian society, and bore a marked Olmec imprint, a state of affairs which we shall find repeated for Tlatilco, in the Valley of Mexico.

The site of Tlatilco

The simple picture of a myriad of 'Neolithic'-looking villages such as that at Chiapa de Corzo scattered over the Mexican countryside without any great social differentiation among them is an over-simplification, as the Oaxaca data suggest. Evidence from excavations in the Valley of Mexico makes clear that some settlements had already taken precedence over others in both social rank and in economic advantage. The key site for the Early Formative in the Valley is Tlatilco, which came to light in 1936 during excavations carried out by brickworkers digging for clay, not, alas, by archaeologists. The visitor to the site today will find nothing but a series of huge holes in the ground, surrounded by factories. In actuality, only a tiny fraction of Tlatilco was ever cleared under scientific conditions.

Settled by about 1200 BC, Tlatilco was a very large village (or small town) sprawling over about 65 hectares. Located to the west of the great lake on a small stream, it was not very far removed from

19 Sub-floor burials with offerings of pottery bottles, bowls, dishes, and figurines at Tlatilco, Early Formative period, 1200–900 BC.

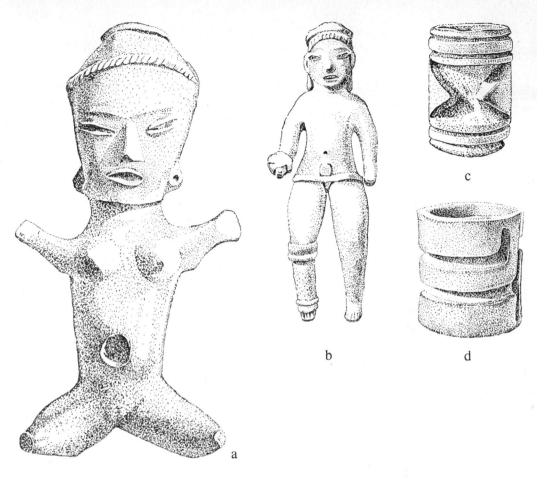

the lakeshore where fishing and the snaring of birds could be pursued. In the Tlatilco refuse are the bones of deer and waterfowl, while represented in the potter's art are armadillo, opossum, wild turkey, bears, frogs, rabbits, fish, ducks, and turtles. Conspicuously present in those parts of the site actually excavated by archaeologists were the outlines of underground, bell-shaped pits. They were filled with dark earth, charcoal, ashes, figurine and pottery fragments, animal bones, and lumps of burned clay from the walls of pole-and-thatch houses; as in Oaxaca, they must have served originally for the storage of grain belonging to various households.

No less than 340 burials were uncovered by archaeologists at Tlatilco, but there must have been many hundreds more destroyed by brickworkers (sometimes at the instigation of unscrupulous collectors). All these were extended skeletons accompanied by the most lavish offerings, especially by figurines which only rarely appear as burial furniture in Formative Mexico.

There are two sorts of figurines: one that is large and hollow, and painted red, and the other small, solid, and of incredibly delicate and sophisticated workmanship. The latter usually represent girls

20 Pottery figurines and roller stamps from Tlatilco. *a* is hollow and bears traces of red, yellow, and white paint; *b* is hollow, was painted red and yellow, and represents a ball player.

19

20

49

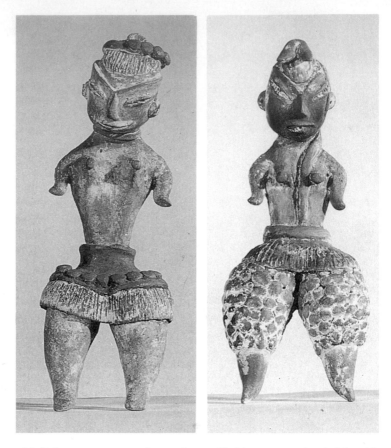

21 Pottery figurine of a dancer, Tlatilco, Valley of Mexico. Early Formative period. Ht 11.4 cm.

22 Pottery figurine of a dancer, Tlatilco, Valley of Mexico. Early Formative period. Ht 12 cm.

21, 22   with little more to wear than paint applied in patterns (probably with the clay roller stamps which have been found in the excavations), although some are attired in what would seem to be grass skirts. Here we encounter males as well, clothed in a simple breechclout. What an extraordinary glimpse of the life of these Formative aristocrats is provided in their figurines! We see women affectionately carrying children or dogs; dancers, some with rattles around the legs; acrobats and contortionists; and matrimonial couples on couches. While no ball courts are known for this period, it nevertheless is certain that the ball game was played, for many figurines show players with the protection for the hand and knee required by that sport.

A distinctly macabre streak appears in the art of the inhabitants of Tlatilco, possessed by a psychological bent that delighted in monstrosities. To illustrate this point, one might mention such representations as two-headed persons, or heads with three eyes, two noses and two mouths; hunchbacks; idiots; horribly ugly and sometimes masked individuals who may be shamans; and many other outrageous deformities. Several actual clay masks have been found, of the most sinister appearance; a few of these are oddly split vertically into two distinct faces, one of which might be a skull, for

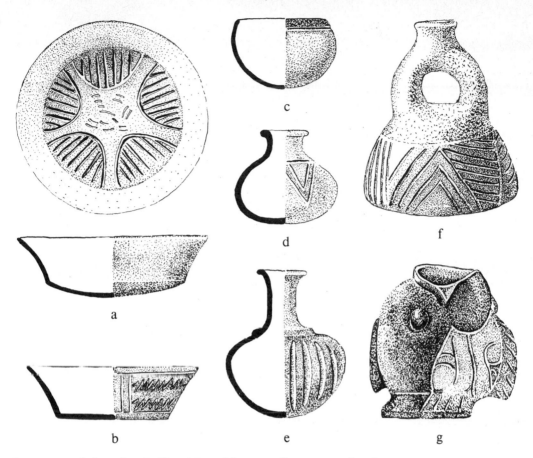

instance, and the other half an idiot with protruding tongue. Let it be noted here that dualism, the unity of basically opposed principles such as life and death, constitutes the very basis of the later religions of Mexico, no matter how great their complexity. Here we see the origin of the concept.

The pottery of Tlatilco bears a vague relation to the later peasant wares of El Arbolillo and Zacatenco, but there the resemblance ends. Within the bounds of the Formative tradition of plastic decoration and the restrained use of color, the potters of this village made ceramics which are among the most aesthetically satisfying ever produced in ancient Mexico. Forms include bowls, neckless jars, long-necked bottles, little spouted trays (possibly for libations), bowls and jars with three tall feet, and, most peculiarly, jars with spouts which resemble stirrups. One or two colors of slip such as red and white are sometimes applied; colors and all kinds of roughening of the surface are confined to definite areas of the vessel by broad, grooved outlines. Particularly favored were contrasting zones of matt and polished surfaces, as well as zoned rocker-stamping. Designs such as stylized jaguar paws were carried out by cutting away part of the surface, the deep areas often filled with bright red pigment after firing.

23 Representative pottery vessels from Tlatilco, Early Formative period. *a*, polished brown bowl with 'sunburst' striations on the interior; *b*, rocker-stamped dish; *c*, red-rimmed bowl; *d–e*, necked jars; *f*, black stirrup-spout jar; *g*, black effigy in the shape of a fish, polished in zones. 1/4.

There was great excitement in archaeological circles when the Tlatilco complex came to light, for something resembling it was already known elsewhere – thousands of miles to the south, in Peru. There also, in the very earliest civilization of the South American continent, the Chavín culture (c. 1100–400 BC), were found such odd pottery shapes as stirrup spouts and long-necked bottles, associated with unusual techniques like rocker-stamping and red-filled excising, as well as roller seals, figurines of Mexican appearance and split-face dualism. A chance resemblance or not?

Earlier editions of this book leaned heavily toward the idea, reminiscent of the old Spinden hypothesis, that such resemblances were the result of Mexican intrusion on the Early Formative level onto the north coast of Peru, but the picture is now less clear. There is an overwhelming body of evidence which points to an independent evolution of ceremonial architecture, art, and therefore civilization in Peru. Further, if there *were* intercontinental diffusion at such an early time, it might well have been cultural spread to both areas from the lowland Pacific coastal area of Ecuador, where such indications of settled life as large villages, ceramics, and maize agriculture extend back beyond 3000 BC. Two recent finds in western Mexico suggest that such was the case. At the site of Capacha, in Colima, Isabel Kelly has unearthed grave goods dating to about 1450 BC which emphasize pottery bottles and stirrup spouts, and which unmistakably point to an Ecuadorian origin; and an elaborate tomb at El Opeño, in Michoacan, has very similar ceramics with a radiocarbon date of about 1300 BC.

On the other hand, it is certain that domestic maize was transmitted to Peru from the north, and only a few South American specialists are opposed to the idea that Early Formative iconography – focused upon the awesome images of the jaguar, cayman, and harpy eagle – was shared through diffusion between the two areas. At this stage of our knowledge, however, it must be admitted that the conclusive evidence bearing on this most important problem of long-range diffusion in the hemisphere has yet to be gathered.

No mention has yet been made of another curious element in the burial offerings of Tlatilco, namely, the very distinct presence of a strange art style known to have originated at the same time in the swampy jungles of the Gulf Coast. This style, called 'Olmec', was produced by the first civilization of Mesoamerica, and its weird iconography which often combined the lineaments of a snarling jaguar with that of a baby is unmistakably apparent in many of the figurines and in much of the pottery. The great expert on the pre-Spanish art of Mexico, Miguel Covarrubias, reasoned that the obviously greater wealth and social superiority of the Tlatilco people over their more simple contemporaries in the Valley of Mexico were the result of an influx of Olmec aristocrats from the eastern lowlands. This may possibly have been so, but it is equally likely that these villagers were a favorably placed people under heavy influence from 'missionaries' spreading the Olmec faith, without a necessary movement of populations. But more about the Olmecs in the next chapter.

Established villages of the Middle Formative

Let us turn now from the Early Formative to the somewhat incomplete information which is at hand for the villages girdling the Valley of Mexico during the middle range (*c.* 900–300 BC) of that period. A word of caution, however – because of our fair knowledge of these sites, the impression has been given that the Valley had more ancient Formative beginnings than elsewhere. On the contrary, that isolated basin was probably a laggard in cultural development until the Classic period, when it became and stayed the flower of Mexican civilization. Notwithstanding its later glory, the Valley was then a prosperous but provincial backwater, which occasionally received new items developed elsewhere.

These Middle Formative villages fringed the placid waters of the great lake, once more fully expanded. From the reed-covered marshes, abounding in waterfowl, across the rich, soft soils in the bottomlands of the Valley, to the forested hills populous with deer, this was an environment favorable in the extreme. Perhaps the surroundings were too bountiful for the stimulation that a people seem to need in order to make real progress: no challenge, and therefore no response, in the scheme of Professor Toynbee.

The first phase at the site of El Arbolillo seems to mark the initial Middle Formative occupation of the Valley. This little village was established directly on the sands of a beach fronting an arm of the great lake. Protected from the chill winds of winter by the slopes of a nearby hill, the farmers drew sustenance from the products of their fields and from the lake. That the village was occupied for many centuries is indicated by the more than 7 m of accumulated midden deposits cut into by the excavator, consisting of refuse, casts of maize leaves, and burned daub fallen from the walls of pole-and-thatch huts.

Zacatenco, another site similarly placed on the edge of the lake, provides further evidence for the intensity of the village-farming life in the Valley. So much refuse was deposited in the Early Zacatenco phase (which follows on the heels of El Arbolillo I), that the villagers were forced to level it from time to time as terraces along which they built their wattle-and-daub houses.

Farmers they were, but the chase also provided much food to the Zacatenco and El Arbolillo peasants, as is well documented in the immense quantities of bones from deer and aquatic birds in their refuse. They hunted with small lance points chipped from obsidian, a hard, black volcanic glass worked with ease. Deer provided not only meat but also hides, which were cleaned of fat with little obsidian scrapers, and bones from which were fashioned awls and bodkins for working baskets and skins. Within each house, the farmer's wife ground the soaked maize on the familiar quern, although for some reason this was absent at El Arbolillo. For cooking and storage, they had a pleasant but undistinguished pottery, usually reddish-brown in color and finely burnished; a somewhat better type was produced at El Arbolillo, little three-legged bowls, smoked black, with red paint rubbed into geometric designs incised on the surface.

At these two sites and elsewhere in the Valley the midden deposits are literally stuffed with thousands of fragments of clay figurines, all female, providing a lively view of the costume of the day, or its lack. Although nudity was apparently the rule, these little ladies have elaborate face and body painting in black, white, and red; headdresses and coiffures as shown were very fancy, wraparound turbans being most common. The technique of manufacture was about like that with which gingerbread men are made, features being indicated by a combination of punching and filleting. Significantly, no recognizable depictions of gods or goddesses have ever been identified in these villages, suggesting the possibility that the only cult was that of the figurines, which may have been objects of household devotion like the Roman *lares*, perhaps concerned with the fertility of the crops.

The dead were buried under the floors of houses, the usual fashion in Mesoamerica, but also occasionally together in cemeteries. With knees drawn up against the chest and wrapped in the mat upon which he had slept in life, the deceased was placed in a simple grave dug in the sand, although sometimes this was outlined and covered by stone slabs. A few pots or implements dropped in the grave, and a jade bead occasionally placed in the mouth (a symbol of life here and in China), tell something of a belief in an existence after death. Child mortality was high, as a good percentage of the skeletons found are of immature individuals.

Late Formative cultures of the central highlands

The Olmec stimulus had been absent from the Valley of Mexico since 900 BC, and cultural development proceeded along its own lines. The isolation of the Valley from what was happening in the rest of Mesoamerica became even more pronounced in the period from 300 BC to AD 150. The mainstream of higher culture in that period was running through the lowlands of eastern Mexico and up the river valleys into the southern highlands and southeastern part of the Republic, ignoring the Valley. This isolation holds true for much of the central highland region, except where direct Olmec intrusions had taken place.

Bright colors and an increase in the size and length of vessel feet were the concern of the potter in Late Formative times. The predilection towards the use of two or more colors in ceramic decoration is well illustrated by Chupícuaro, the burial ground of a village which lay above the Lerma River in the state of Guanajuato, about 80 miles northwest of the Valley of Mexico: While the Chupícuaro complex is widespread in the region, until recent excavations it was known, like Tlatilco, only from commercial pot-hunting. The skeletons of 390 individuals were found, almost all of whom had been laid on their backs in simple graves with abundant offerings of pottery, figurines, jade, and various clay objects. The later Mexicans believed that the owner's dog would help his soul across their equivalent of the Styx, and we find at Chupícuaro that dogs were also interred, many of them with great

care. The pottery vessels found in the cemetery are in both shape and decoration quite exuberant. In form one encounters bowls with all sorts of supports: short tripods, very long and attenuated tripods, swollen feet in the shape of breasts, pedestal bases. There are a few stirrup-spout jars, the last time this odd type is seen in Mexico, although it continued to enjoy great popularity in Peru until Colonial days. Vessel painting is lively, the slips used most often being red on buff, red and black on buff, or red and brown on buff, in finely proportioned, abstract designs which appear to have been derived from textiles. Little handmade, clay figurines of the 'pretty lady' type were likewise dropped into the graves; these are charming and quite nude, with slanting eyes and fancy coiffures built up from clay strips.

The most notable advance in the Late Formative of central Mexico was the appearance of the temple-pyramid. The earliest temples of the highlands were thatch-roof, perishable structures not unlike the houses of the common people, erected within the community on low earthen platforms faced with sun-hardened clay. There are a few slight indications that some such platforms once existed at Tlatilco. By the Late Formative, however, they had become almost universal, as the nuclei of enlarged villages and even towns. Towards the end of the period, clay facings for the platforms were occasionally replaced by retaining-walls of undressed stones coated with a thick layer of stucco, and the substructures themselves had become greatly enlarged, sometimes rising in several stages or tiers. Here we have, then, a definite progression from small villages of farmers with but household figurine cults, to hierarchical societies with rulers who could call the populace to build and maintain sizeable religious establishments.

24 Polychrome tripod jar, Chupícuaro culture, Guanajuato. Late Formative period. Ht 14 cm.

25 Pottery figurine of the 'pretty lady' type, Chupícuaro culture, Guanajuato. Late Formative period. Ht about 10 cm.

25

26 View west of a portion of the circular temple platform at Cuicuilco, Valley of Mexico. Late Formative period.

26

How grandiose some of these substructures were can be seen at Cuicuilco, located to the south of Mexico City near the National University, in an area covered by the *Pedregal* – a grim landscape of broken, soot-black lava with a sparse flora eking out its existence in rocky crevices. The principal feature of Cuicuilco is a round platform, 118 m in diameter and rising in four inwardly sloping tiers to a present height of 23 m. Two ramps placed on either side of the platform provide access to the summit, which was crowned at one time by a cone-like construction which brought the total height to about 27 m. Faced with volcanic rocks, the interior of the surviving structure is filled with sand and rubble, with a total volume of 60,000 cubic meters.

It is little wonder that Cuicuilco was once thought to be of hoary antiquity, for the main structure, excavated many years ago, is surrounded and partly covered by lava which had flowed down from Xictli volcano, looming on the western horizon above the Valley floor. Estimates varying anywhere from 8,500 to 30,000 years were made for the age of the flow by competent authorities. But this was in the pre-radiocarbon era, and long prior to Vaillant's careful work on the cultural stratigraphy of the Valley.

On the grounds of the associated ceramics and figurines, quantities of which are found beneath the *Pedregal*, Cuicuilco is clearly Late Formative, as confirmed by C14 dates. The doom of Cuicuilco was set some time around AD 100, an end which must have been spectacular. The young Xictli first sent out dust and ashes which fell in quantity on the site, then the great eruptions themselves began, molten lava pouring out over the southwestern margin of the Valley. All must have fled in panic from the region. Did the inhabitants have any premonitions of the final cataclysm? One might

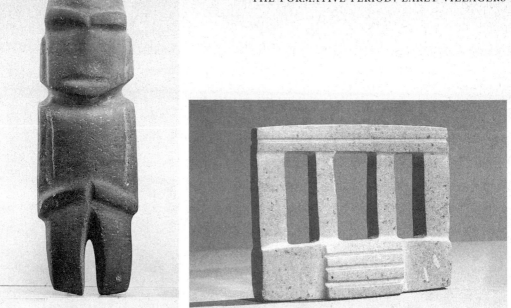

think so, for prominent among the remains of their culture are clay incense burners in the form of Xiuhtecuhtli, who was Fire God and lord of the volcanoes among the ancient Mexicans.

In lieu of extensive excavations underneath the lava, it is difficult to be precise about the size and function of a regional center like Cuicuilco. On the basis of his unrivaled knowledge of the Valley of Mexico, however, William Sanders ascribes to it a population of 20,000, the chief center of a total Valley population of perhaps 140,000 souls. Regardless of the uncertainty about Cuicuilco, it surely presaged the great Teotihuacan civilization of the Classic period.

27 Standing figure of stone, Mezcala style, Guerrero. Late Formative period. Ht 32 cm.

28 Stone model of a temple, Mezcala style, Guerrero. Late Formative period. Ht 12 cm.

The Mezcala puzzle

Although a rich source for portable jade objects in Olmec style, the rather dry basin of the upper Balsas or Mezcala River, in the state of Guerrero, is one of the archaeologically least known regions in Mexico. During the Middle and Late Formative, and perhaps developing out of an Olmec substratum, appears the style called Mezcala, known only from carved pieces of andesite and serpentine recovered by illegal excavations. These objects are highly abstract, usually representations of human figures recalling in pose and technique the simpler small productions of Teotihuacan, which they may foreshadow. As well as these, miniature façades of colonnaded temples are also known, and a few effigies of natural objects like conch shells.

27

28

The exact dating and cultural context of Mezcala art will only be known when scientific excavation is undertaken in the area. Large-scale looting of Mezcala mounds is now known to go all the way back to the Aztecs, as many Mezcala objects were recovered in dedicatory caches found in recent investigations of the Great Temple of Tenochtitlan, as we shall see in Chapter 9.

The shaft-tomb art of western Mexico

Nayarit, Jalisco, and Colima are three contiguous states on the Pacific Coast between Guerrero and the Gulf of California. Here, a number of local centers produced a surprising range of art in clay, some of it showing a lively sense of humor. Some of these handmade figures and vessels were once thought to be Classic in date on the ground of a certain tenuous resemblance of some forms to Teotihuacan pottery, but in spite of our abysmal ignorance of the prehistory of the area, most archaeologists now believe that they were produced during the Late Formative. It is also believed that all were looted from chamber tombs reached from the surface by shafts up to 6 m or more in depth. Needless to say, those tombs seen by archaeologists had already been cleared of their contents. Some of these tombs consist of multiple chambers, suggesting vaults which were used by families or lineages over long periods.

Nayarit, particularly the neighborhood around Ixtlan del Río, specialized in lively figures and groups painted in black, white, and yellow on a reddish ground. The subjects are men and women in naturalistic poses, some playing flutes or beating turtle-shell drums;

30

29 Pottery house group from Ixtlan del Río, Nayarit. The circular 'floor' has a diameter of 53 cm. The exact chronological placement of this, like almost all western Mexican hand-modeled figures and groups, is unknown but is probably Late Formative. Here we see four thatch-roof houses on platforms arranged around a plaza, in the center of which is a four-tiered, circular temple-pyramid. Among the fifty figures are musicians playing trumpets and rasps, a pair of lovers, water carriers, children, dogs, and five men attempting to seduce a woman.

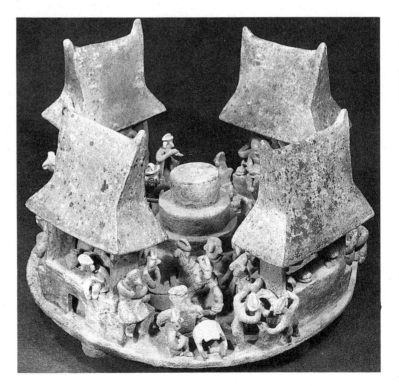

30 (*left*) Pottery figure of a man striking a turtle-shell with a deer antler, from Nayarit. The face and body have been decorated with polychrome paints. Percussion instruments of this sort are still in use in remote villages of Mexico. Probably Late Formative period. Ht 38 cm.

31 (*above*) Seated person holding a dish, pottery, from Jalisco, western Mexico. Probably Late Formative period. Ht 51 cm.

32 (*left*) Hunchback dwarf, pottery, from Colima, western Mexico. Late Formative period. Ht 86 cm.

29   warriors brandishing clubs; temples with thatched roofs; two-storied houses and even villages; and ball courts with the game actually going on. Although artistically of little note, the realistic nature of the scenes renders them of great ethnological interest, for much of the everyday life of ancient Mexico is here revealed in startling detail.

31   A more sophisticated and polished art in clay was produced by Jalisco and Colima. Especially famous are the little pot-bellied dogs of Colima belonging to the hairless breed that the Mexicans specially fattened for consumption by forced feeding like Strasbourg geese; these are depicted sleeping, playing, growling, and in
32   many other moods. Other vessels represent various kinds of birds, hunchbacks, warriors, and all the variety of human life that interested these potters, including occasional pornography (a rarity in Mexican art). Particularly attractive are the red ware pots enclosed by water-lily petals, borne by legs in the form of birds or atlantean humans.

An earlier school of thought held that this shaft-tomb sculpture was little more than a kind of genre art: realistic, anecdotal, and with no more religious meaning than a Dutch interior. This view has been vigorously challenged by the ethnologist Peter Furst, who has worked closely with the contemporary Huichol Indians of Nayarit, almost certainly the descendants of the people who made the tomb figures. Among the Huichol and their close relatives, the Cora, religious practitioners are always shamans, powerful specialists who effect cures and maintain the well-being of their people by battling against demons and evil shamans. Professor Furst noted that the warriors with clubs from Nayarit and Jalisco tombs are down on one knee, the typical fighting stance of the shaman. The Nayarit house models are interpreted by him not just as two-storey village dwellings, but as chthonic dwellings of the dead: above would be the house of the living, below is the house of the dead. Such a belief is consonant not only with Huichol ideas about death and the soul, but also with the supernatural concepts of Southwestern Indians like the Hopi.

The Furst hypothesis that the symbolism of shaft-tomb art 'conforms closely to characteristically shamanistic initiatory, funerary, and death-and-rebirth beliefs and rituals' is entirely logical considering the funerary context of this sculpture. Dogs, as we have seen with Chupícuaro, had a special mortuary significance in ancient Mexico, and one fine Colima example even wears a human mask – perhaps the face of his master! The seeming realism of this art is deceptive, and we still have much to learn about it.

5
The Formative period: early civilizations

Background of civilized life

The advance in the arts and technology that is implied by the word 'civilization' is usually involved with the idea of urbanism. Nonetheless, the evidence is equivocal or negative for the presence of true cities among some Old and New World civilizations. One learns to one's surprise that such were missing among the Cambodians and Mycenaeans, and it is still debatable whether the great Classic Maya centers were really cities.

Writing is another criterion of civilized life, but of course it should be remembered that the large and complex Inca empire had no writing at all, but relied instead on the *quipu*, or knot record, for administrative purposes. However, most, if not all, the peoples of Mesoamerica eventually developed systems of writing; the Maya took this trait to its highest degree of development, with a mixed semantic-phonetic script in which they apparently could write anything they wished. As we shall see, Mesoamerican writing has very early origins, appearing in a few areas by the middle or end of the Formative period.

'By their works ye shall know them', and archaeologists tend to judge cultures as civilizations by the presence of great public works and unified, evolved, monumental art styles. Life became organized under the direction of an élite class, usually strengthened by writing and other techniques of bureaucratic administration. Early civilizations were qualitatively different from the tribal cultures which preceded them, and with which in some cases they co-existed. The kind of art produced by them reveals the sort of compulsive force which held together these first civilized societies, namely, a state religion in which the political leaders were the intermediaries between gods and men. The monumental sculpture of these ancient peoples therefore tends to be loaded with religious symbolism, calculated to strike awe in the breast of the beholder.

Unless the written record is extraordinarily explicit, which it seldom is in Mesoamerica except for the Classic Maya and the Late Post-Classic peoples of central Mexico, it is extremely difficult to detect the first appearance of the state from archaeological evidence alone. A state is characterized not only by a centralized bureaucratic apparatus in the hands of an élite class, but also by the element of coercion: a standing army and usually a police force.

Mesoamerican archaeology provides plentiful data on the emergence of élite, high status groups, but not very much on warfare or internal control, although both were surely present for over 2,000 years prior to the arrival of the Spaniards. Thus, in the absence of extensive written records, the argument over whether peoples like the Olmec had true states may never be resolved.

Many of the later cultures of Mesoamerica were only weakly urban. The basic form of settlement pattern was what might be called the 'élite center', an architectural cluster in which lived the rulers and the priestly hierarchies, along with all their retainers, with the great mass of the people in hamlets and villages scattered through the countryside. Such a pattern could only have worked if the rulers could have called on the surrounding peasantry as corvée labor to build and maintain the temples and palaces, and for food to support the non-farming specialists, whether kings, priests, or artisans. In conjunction with an elaborate ritual and civic calendar, writing sprang up early to ensure the proper operation of this process, and to celebrate great events in the life of the élite. Furthermore, in these centers were held at regular intervals the markets in which all sorts of food and manufactures of hinterland and center changed hands. This is the basic Mesoamerican pattern, established in the Formative, and persisting until Conquest times in many areas.

The Olmec civilization

The most ancient Mexican civilization is that called 'Olmec'. For many years, archaeologists had known about small jade sculptures and other objects in a distinct and powerful style that emphasized human infants with snarling, jaguar-like features. Most of these could be traced to the sweltering Gulf Coast plain, the region of southern Veracruz and neighboring Tabasco, just west of the Maya area. George Vaillant recognized the fundamental unity of all these works, and assigned them to the 'Olmecs', the mysterious 'rubber people' described by Sahagún as inhabiting jungle country of the Gulf Coast; thus the name became established.

33

Actually, nothing is known of the real people who produced Olmec art, neither the name that they called themselves by nor from where they came. Old poems in Nahuatl, recorded after the Conquest, speak of a legendary land called Tamoanchan, on the eastern sea, settled long before the founding of Teotihuacan

> in a certain era
> which no one can reckon
> which no one can remember,

where

> there was a government for a long time.[1]

This tradition is intriguing, for Tamoanchan is not a good Nahuatl name but Mayan, meaning 'Land of Rain or Mist'. It will be recalled that an isolated Mayan language, Huastec, is still spoken in

33 Jade effigy ax, known as the 'Kunz' ax. The combination of carving, drilling, and incising seen on this piece is characteristic of the Olmec style. Olmec culture, Middle Formative period, provenience unknown. Ht 28 cm.

northern Veracruz. One possibility is that there was an unbroken band of Mayan speech extending along the Gulf Coast all the way from the Maya area proper to the Huasteca, and that the region in which the Olmec civilization was established could have been in those distant times Mayan-speaking. This would suggest that the Olmec homeland was the real Tamoanchan, and that the original 'Olmecs' spoke a Mayan tongue.

In contradiction to this hypothesis, some compelling evidence has been advanced by the linguists Lyle Campbell and Terence Kaufman strongly suggesting that the Olmec spoke an ancestral form of Mixe-Zoquean. There are a large number of Mixe-Zoquean loan words in other Mesoamerican languages, including Mayan. Most of these are words, such as *pom* ('copal incense'), associated with high-status activities and ritual typical of early civilization. Although the dominant language of the Olmec area was until recently a form of Nahua, this is generally believed to be a relatively late arrival; on the other hand, Popoloca, a member of the Mixe-Zoquean family, is still spoken along the eastern slopes of the Tuxtla Mountains, in the very region from which the Olmec obtained the basalt for their monuments. Since the Olmec were the great, early, culture-bearing force in Mesoamerica, the case for Mixe-Zoquean is very strong.

(*Opposite*)
34 Greenstone figure from
Las Limas, Veracruz. A
young man or adolescent boy
holds the figure of an infant
were-jaguar deity in his
arms, while his shoulders
and knees are incised with
the heads of four other
deities. Olmec culture,
Middle Formative period. Ht
55 cm.

35 Deity heads incised on the
shoulders and knees of the
Las Limas sculpture.

There has been much controversy about the dating of the Olmec
civilization. Its discoverer, the late Matthew Stirling, consistently
held that it predated the Classic Maya civilization, a position which
was vehemently opposed by such Mayanists as Sir Eric Thompson.
Stirling was backed by the great Mexican scholars Alfonso Caso
and Miguel Covarrubias, who held for a placement in the Formative
period, largely on the grounds that Olmec traits had appeared in
sites of that period in the Valley of Mexico and in the state of
Morelos. Time has fully borne out Stirling and the Mexican school.
A long series of radiocarbon dates from the important Olmec site of
La Venta spans the centuries from 900 to 400 BC, placing the major
development of this center entirely within the Middle Formative.
Another set of dates shows that the site of San Lorenzo is even
older, falling within the Early Formative (1200 to 900 BC), making it
contemporary with Tlatilco and other highland sites in which
influence from San Lorenzo can be detected. There is now not the
slightest doubt that all later civilizations in Mesoamerica, whether
Mexican or Maya, ultimately rest on an Olmec base.

The hallmark of Olmec civilization is the art style. Its most
unusual aspect is the iconography on which it is based, through
which we glimpse a religion of the strangest sort. The Olmec
evidently believed that at some distant time in the past, a woman
had cohabited with a jaguar, this union giving rise to a race of
were-jaguars, combining the lineaments of felines and men. These
monsters are usually shown in Olmec art as somewhat infantile
throughout life, with the puffy features of small, fat babies, snarling
mouths, toothless gums or long, curved fangs, and even claws. The
heads are cleft at the top, perhaps representing some congenital
abnormality like *spina bifida*. Were-jaguars are always quite sexless,
with the obesity of eunuchs. In one way or another, the concept of
the were-jaguar is at the heart of the Olmec civilization. What were
these creatures in function?

Covarrubias, an artist-archaeologist with a profound feeling for
Mesoamerican art styles, developed an ingenious scheme purport-
ing to show that all the various rain gods of the Classic and
Post-Classic cultures could be derived from an Olmec were-jaguar
prototype, a somewhat implausible hypothesis since the Olmec area
is one of the rainiest in Mexico and could have had little need for
such a supreme deity. The chance find of a large greenstone figure
near the village of Las Limas, Veracruz, shows that Olmec
iconography was far more complex. This figure represents an
adolescent boy or young man, holding in his arms a were-jaguar
baby, a theme also to be seen on some Olmec 'altars'. Incised on
both shoulders and both knees are the profile heads of four Olmec
gods; each of them has distinctive iconographic features, although
all four have cleft heads.

Following the lead of the Las Limas figure, David Joralemon has
been able to show that the Olmec worshipped a variety of deities,
only a few of whom exhibit the features of the jaguar. Just as
prominent in their pantheon were such awesome lowland creatures
as the cayman and harpy eagle, and fearsome sea creatures like the

34

35

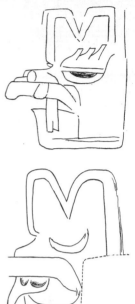

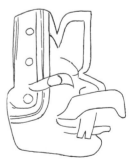

shark. These were combined in a multitude of forms which bewilder the modern beholder.

Given its odd content, Olmec art is nevertheless 'realistic' and shows a great mastery of form. On the great basalt monuments of the Olmec 'heartland' and in other sculptures, scenes which include what are apparently portraits of real persons are present; many of these are bearded, some with aquiline features. Olmec bas-reliefs are notable in the use of empty space in compositions. The combination of tension in space and the slow rhythm of the lines, which are always curved, produces the overwhelmingly monumental character of the style, no matter how small the object.

The Olmec were above all carvers of stone, from the really gigantic Colossal Heads, stelae, and altars of the Veracruz-Tabasco region, to finely carved jade celts, figurines, and pendants. Typical is a combination of carving, drilling (using a reed and wet sand), and delicate incising. Olmec sculptures are usually three-dimensional, to be seen from all sides, not just from the front. Very small sculptures and figurines of a beautiful blue-green jade and of serpentine were, of course, portable, so that we are not always sure of the place of origin of many of these pieces. Olmec objects of small size have been found all over Mexico, especially in the state of Guerrero in the western part of the Republic, but most of these could have been carried thence by aboriginal trade or even by

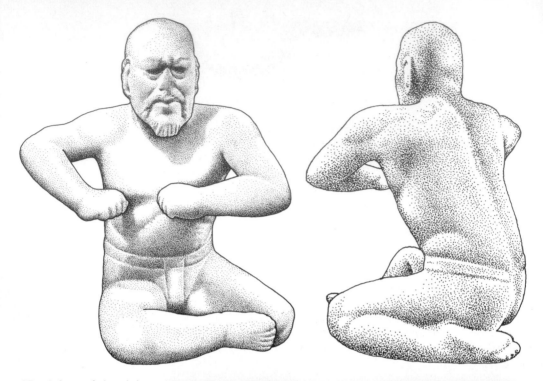

36 Basalt figure of a bearded man, the so-called 'Wrestler'. Olmec culture, Early or Middle Formative period, Arroyo Sonso, Veracruz. Ht 66 cm.

37 Small stone figure of a woman and child, provenience unknown. Olmec culture, Middle Formative period. Ht 11.4 cm.

Olmec missionaries. Among these are magnificent effigy axes of jade, basalt, or other stone, some of which are so thin and completely useless as axes that they must have had a ritual purpose. The were-jaguar is on many of these, sometimes inclining towards the feline, sometimes more anthropomorphic, along with other Olmec deities. The Olmec style was also represented in pottery bowls and figurines, and even in wood (in a miraculously preserved mask with jade incrustations from a cave in Guerrero).

38

The region of southern Veracruz and neighboring Tabasco has been justifiably called the Olmec 'heartland'. Here is where the great Olmec sites and Olmec monuments are concentrated, and here is where the myth represented in Olmec art appears in its most elaborate form. There is hardly any question that the civilization had its roots and its highest development in that zone, which is little more than 125 miles long by about 50 miles wide. The heartland is characterized by a very high annual rainfall (over 300 cm) and, before the advent of the white man, by a very high, tropical forest cover, interspersed with savannahs. Much of it is alluvial lowland, formed by the many rivers which meet the Gulf of Mexico near by. The so-called 'dry season' of the heartland is hardly that, for during the winters cold, wet northers sweep down from the north, keeping the soil moist for year-round cultivation. It was in this seemingly inhospitable environment that the New World's first civilization was produced.

38 Wooden mask, encrusted with jade, supposedly from a cave near Iguala, Guerrero. Olmec culture, Middle Formative period. Ht 19 cm.

(*Opposite*)
39 Monument 17, San
Lorenzo, Veracruz, shortly
after excavation. One of the
smaller Colossal Heads,
wearing the typical 'football
helmet'. The nearest source
of the basalt from which this
was carved lies more than 50
miles to the north. Olmec
culture, Early Formative
period. Ht 1.67 m.

40 Monument 4, San
Lorenzo, Veracruz. Olmec
culture, Early Formative
period. Ht 1.78 m.

41 Monument 2, Potrero
Nuevo (a subsidiary site of
San Lorenzo), Veracruz.
Two atlantean dwarfs
support the top of this basalt
'altar', which probably served
as a throne. Olmec culture,
Early Formative period. Ht
94 cm.

The San Lorenzo Olmec

Credit for the discovery of the Olmec civilization goes to Stirling, who explored and excavated Tres Zapotes, La Venta, and San Lorenzo during the 1930s and 1940s. In 1945, he and his wife Marion were led to the site of San Lorenzo by a report of a stone eye looking up from a trail. They realized that this belonged to one of the Colossal Heads typical of Olmec culture, and excavated the site through two field seasons, during which they discovered a wealth of sculpture, much of it lying in or near the ravines which surround San Lorenzo. However, they were able to date neither the sculpture nor the site itself.

Convinced that San Lorenzo might hold the key to the origin of Olmec civilization, I directed a Yale archaeological–ecological project there from 1966 to 1968. San Lorenzo is the most important of a cluster of three sites lying near the flat bottoms of the Coatzacoalcos River, not very far from the center of the heartland. When we had mapped it, it turned out to be a kind of plateau rising about 50 m above the surrounding lowlands; about three-quarters of a mile long in a north–south direction, excavations proved it to be artificial down to a depth of 7 m, with long ridges jutting out on its northwest, west, and south sides. Mirror symmetry is characteristic of San Lorenzo, so that a particular feature on one ridge is mimicked on its counterpart. It is difficult to imagine what the Olmec meant by this gigantic construction of earth, clay, and other materials brought up on the backs of the peasantry, but it is possible that they meant this to be a huge animal effigy, possibly a bird flying east, but never completed because of the destruction of the site.

San Lorenzo had first been settled about 1500 BC, but by 1200 BC had become thoroughly Olmec. At its height, some of the most magnificent and awe-inspiring sculptures ever discovered in Mexico were fashioned without the benefit of metal tools; petrographic analysis showed this to be basalt which had been quarried from boulders on the volcanic Cerro Cintepec, in the Tuxtla Mountains, a straight-line distance away of 50 miles. Presumably the stones were dragged down to navigable streams and loaded on great balsa rafts, then floated first down to the coast of the Gulf of Mexico, then up the Coatzacoalcos River, from whence they would have had to be dragged, probably with rollers, up to the San Lorenzo plateau. The amount of labor which must have been involved staggers the imagination.

The Early Formative sculptures of San Lorenzo include eight Colossal Heads of great distinction. These are up to 2.85 m in height and weigh many tons; it is believed that they are all portraits of mighty Olmec rulers, with thick-lipped 'Negroid' features. They wear headgear rather like American football helmets which probably served as protection in both war and in the ceremonial game played with a rubber ball throughout Mesoamerica. Indeed, we found not only figurines of ball players at San Lorenzo, but also a simple, earthen court constructed for the game. Also typical are the so-called 'altars': large basalt blocks with flat tops which may weigh

39

40

up to 40 metric tons. The fronts of these altars have niches in which sits the figure of a ruler, either holding a were-jaguar baby in his arms (probably the theme of royal descent) or holding a rope which binds captives (the theme of warfare and conquest), depicted in relief on the sides. Rather than actually serving as altars, David Grove has demonstrated that they must have been thrones. One of San Lorenzo's finest 'altars' was found near the satellite site of Potrero Nuevo, and depicts two pot-bellied, atlantean dwarfs supporting the 'altar' top with their upraised hands.

41

In his work at San Lorenzo, Stirling had come across trough-shaped basalt stones which he hypothesized were fitted end-to-end to form a kind of aqueduct. In 1967, we actually came across and excavated such a system in situ. This deeply buried drain line was in the southwestern portion of the site, and consisted of 170 m of laboriously pecked-out stone troughs fitted with basalt covers; three subsidiary lines met it from above at intervals. We have reason to believe that a drain system symmetrical to this exists on the southeastern side of San Lorenzo, and that both served periodically to remove the water from ceremonial pools on the surface of the plateau. Evidence for drains has been found at other Olmec centers, such as La Venta and Laguna de los Cerros, and must have been a feature of Olmec ritual life.

42

Large quantities of household debris came from our San Lorenzo phase levels, including pottery bowls and dishes carved with Olmec designs, beautiful Olmec figurines and fragments of white-ware were-jaguar 'babies', and small mirrors, some of them convex, polished from iron-ore nodes which had perhaps been traded in from distant areas like highland Oaxaca. We recovered thousands of obsidian artifacts, mostly razor-like blades but also dart-points and bone-working tools; there is no natural obsidian in the Gulf Coast heartland, but trace-element analysis showed this

42 Part of a deeply buried drain line, formed of U-shaped troughs placed end-to-end and fitted with covers. The entire line is made of basalt brought in from the Tuxtla Mountains. Olmec culture, San Lorenzo, Early Formative period.

material to have been imported from many sources in highland Mexico and Guatemala, testifying to immense trade networks then controlled by the rising Olmec state.

We found no preserved plant remains, but occasional pockets of midden contained mammal, fish, and amphibian remains. The San Lorenzo Olmec were only slightly interested in hunting of deer and peccary. The mainstays of their diet were fish such as the snook, and domestic dog. Human bones showing butchering and burn marks were also plentiful, an indication of their cannibalistic propensities. There were also a high number of bones from the marine toad (*Bufo marinus*), a creature which is inedible because of the poison in its skin, but perhaps utilized for its production of bufotenine, a known hallucinogen.

From our ecological studies, we have discovered a great deal about the economic basis of early Olmec civilization along the middle Coatzacoalcos. The bulk of the people were maize farmers, raising two crops a year on the more upland soils where rainy-season inundations do not reach; today, these lands are held communally. In contrast, the Olmec élite must have seized for themselves the rich river levees, where bumper crops are secured after the summer floods have subsided. The rise of the first Mesoamerican state, dominated by a hereditary élite class with judicial, military, and religious power, seems to have been the result of two factors: first, an environment with very high agricultural potential due to year-round rains and wet-season inundations of the river margins, along with abundant fish resources; and second, differential access to the best land by crystallizing social groups. The parallel with ancient Egypt – the 'gift of the Nile' – is obvious.

There was nothing egalitarian about San Lorenzo society, as the Colossal Heads testify. The nature of the controls and compulsion required to build the great plateau and transport the monuments eventually led to a mighty cataclysm. About 900 BC San Lorenzo was destroyed either by invasion or revolution, or a combination of these. The grandiose monuments glorifying its rulers and gods were ruthlessly smashed and defaced, then ritually buried in long lines within the ridges, from which some of them (those seen by Stirling) eventually eroded out and tumbled into the ravines. Thanks to the ability of the cesium magnetometer to detect buried basalt, and to the good luck that attended our expedition, we found some of these buried lines, including a magnificent but decapitated figure of a half-kneeling figure of an ancient ballplayer. The fury of the destructive force visited upon these stones astounded us, for in some respects it matched the labor and ingenuity which went into their creation. Civilizations went out with a bang, not a whimper, in early Mesoamerica.

The Olmec of La Venta

After the downfall of San Lorenzo, its power passed to La Venta, Tabasco, one of the greatest of all Olmec sites although now largely demolished by oil operations. It is located on an island in a sea-level coastal swamp near the Tonalá River, about 18 miles inland from the Gulf. The island has slightly more than 2 square miles of dry land. The site itself is in the northern half, and is a linear complex of clay constructions stretched out for 1½ miles in a north–south direction; it has been extensively excavated, before its desecration by air strips, bulldozers, and parking lots, first by Matthew Stirling of the Smithsonian Institution and later by the University of California. The major feature at La Venta is a huge, volcano-shaped, pyramid of clay, 34 m high. The idea behind such enormous mounds is of interest here, for this is the largest of its period in Mexico. It is almost as though man were struggling to get closer to the gods, to raise his temples to the sky. This cannot have been their only function, however, for inside many Mesoamerican pyramids have been found elaborate tombs, made during construction of the pyramids themselves, so that it is likely that the temple-pyramid was an outgrowth of the ancient idea of a burial mound or funerary monument. Whether this is so in the case of the La Venta pyramid we do not know, for although still extant it has never been penetrated.

To the north of the Great Pyramid are two long, low mounds on either side of the center-line, and a low mound in the center between these. Then, one comes to a broad, rectangular court or plaza which was once surrounded by a fence of basalt columns, each over 2 m tall, set side by side in the top of a low wall made of adobe bricks. Finally, along the center-line, is a large, terraced clay mound. There are some who believe that the layout of the main portion of the site represents a gigantic, abstract jaguar mask.

Robert Heizer calculated that this élite center must have been supported by a hinterland population of at least 18,000 persons; the main pyramid alone probably took some 800,000 man-days to construct. He and his colleague Philip Drucker once wrote that the nearest arable land was an area between the Coatzacoalcos and

43 Reconstruction of Complex A, the major ceremonial mound cluster at La Venta.

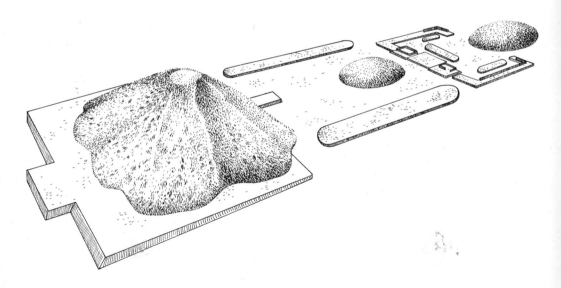

Tonalá Rivers, and that it was on this that the rulers of La Venta depended for food and labor. However, this land is relatively poor and eroded, so that it is far more likely that the agricultural base consisted of the Tonalá levee lands, never examined by them.

In its heyday, the site must have been vastly impressive, for different colored clays were used for floors, and the sides of platforms were painted in solid colors of red, yellow, and purple. Scattered in the plazas fronting these rainbow-hued structures were a large number of monuments sculptured from basalt. Outstanding among these are the Colossal Heads, of which four were found at La Venta. Large stelae (tall, flat monuments) of the same material were also present. Particularly outstanding is Stela 3, dubbed 'Uncle Sam' by archaeologists. On it, two elaborately garbed men face each other, both wearing fantastic headdresses. The figure on the right has a long, aquiline nose and a goatee. Over the two float chubby were-jaguars brandishing war clubs. Also typical are the so-called 'altars'. The finest is Altar 5, on which the central figure emerges from the niche holding a jaguar-baby in his arms; on the sides, four subsidiary adult figures hold other little were-jaguars, who are squalling and gesticulating in a lively manner. As usual, their heads are cleft, and mouths drawn down in the Olmec snarl.

44 North end of Altar 5, La Venta, Tabasco. The two adult figures carry were-jaguar babies with cleft heads. Olmec culture, Middle Formative period. Overall height of the monument 94 cm.

44

45 Offering No. 4 at La
Venta, a cache of sixteen
figurines of jade and
serpentine and six jade celts,
arranged in the form of a
scene. Olmec culture,
Middle Formative period.
Height of figurines varies
from 16 to 18 cm.

A number of buried offerings, perhaps dedicatory, were encountered by the excavators at the site. These usually include quantities
of jade or serpentine celts laid carefully in rows; many of these were
finely incised with were-jaguar and other figures. A particularly
spectacular offering comprised a group of six celts and sixteen
standing figurines of serpentine and jade arranged upright in a sort
of scene. In some offerings were found finely polished ear flares of
jade with attached jade pendants in the outline of jaguar teeth.
Certain Olmec sculptures and figurines show persons wearing
pectorals of concave shape around the neck, and such have actually
come to light in offerings. These turned out to be concave mirrors
of magnetite and ilmenite, the reflecting surfaces polished to optical
specifications. What were they used for? Experiments have shown
that they can not only start fires, but also throw images on flat
surfaces like a *camera lucida.* They were pierced for suspension, and
one can imagine the hocus-pocus which some mighty Olmec priest
was able to perform with one of these.

46 Three rectangular pavements, each about 4.5 by 6 m, are known
at La Venta. Each consists of about 485 blocks of serpentine, laid
out in the form of a highly abstract jaguar mask. Certain details
were left open and emphasized by filling with colored clays. Strange
as it may seem, these were also offerings, as they were covered up
with many feet of clay and adobe layers soon after construction.

In the acid soil of La Venta (as at San Lorenzo), bones disappear quickly, and very few burials have been discovered. Of those found, however, the most outstanding was the tomb in Mound A-2, surrounded and roofed with basalt columns. On a floor made of flat limestone slabs were laid the remains of two juveniles, badly rotted when discovered, each wrapped up in a bundle and heavily coated with vermilion paint. With them had been placed an offering of fine jade figurines, beads, a jade pendant in the shape of a clam shell, a sting-ray spine of the same substance, and other objects. Outside the tomb a sandstone 'sarcophagus' with a cover had been left, but other than some jade objects on the bottom, nothing was found within but clay fill. It could be that the children or infants in the tomb were monstrosities who to the Olmecs may have resembled were-jaguars and thus merited such treatment.

Like the earlier San Lorenzo, La Venta was deliberately destroyed in ancient times. Its fall was certainly violent, as twenty-four out of forty sculptured monuments were intentionally mutilated. This probably occurred at the end of Middle Formative times, around 400–300 BC, for subsequently, following its abandonment as a center, offerings were made with pottery of Late Formative cast. As a matter of fact, La Venta may never have lost its significance as a cult center, for among the very latest caches found was a Spanish olive jar of the early Colonial period, and Professor Heizer suspected that offerings may have been made in modern times as well.

47

46 Mosaic pavement of serpentine blocks, representing an abstract jaguar mask, one of three known at La Venta. The pavement was covered over with a layer of mottled pink clay and a platform of adobe bricks. Olmec culture, Middle Formative period.

47 Tomb constructed of basalt pillars, La Venta, Tabasco. The tomb contained several burials accompanied by jade offerings and was covered with an earthen mound. Olmec culture, Middle Formative period.

Tres Zapotes and the Long Count calendar

In its day, La Venta was undoubtedly the most powerful and holy place in the Olmec heartland, sacred because of its very inaccessibility; but other great Olmec centers also flourished in the Middle Formative. About 100 miles northwest of La Venta lies Tres Zapotes, in a setting of low hills above the swampy basin formed by the Papaloapan and San Juan Rivers. It comprises about fifty earthen mounds stretched out along the bank of a stream for 2 miles. Pottery and clay figurines recovered from stratigraphic excavations have revealed an early occupation of Tres Zapotes which was apparently contemporaneous with La Venta, and a later occupation which post-dated the fall of that great center. Belonging to this earlier, purely Olmec, horizon are two Colossal Heads like those of La Venta. But the importance of Tres Zapotes lies in its famous stela, discussed below.

Thus far we have said nothing about writing and the calendar in the Olmec heartland. Actually, no inscriptions or written dates have come to light at La Venta itself. Nonetheless, several fine jade objects in the Olmec style, now in public and private collections but of unknown provenance, are incised with hieroglyphs. Although unreadable to us, some of them appear to be ancestral to certain Maya glyphs. If they can be assigned to the Middle Formative horizon – and there seems to be no valid reason not to consider them of that age – then these inscriptions mark the very beginnings of writing in Mexico; but the evidence for this is weak.

It has already been said that Tres Zapotes survived into the Late Formative, after La Venta had been overthrown. Tres Zapotes has produced one of the oldest dated monuments of the New World, Stela C, a fragmentary basalt monument which had been re-used in later times. On one side is a very abstract were-jaguar mask in a style which is *derivative* from Olmec, but not in the true canon. The reverse side bears a date in the Long Count.

The Long Count system of calculating dates needs some explanation. In Chapter 1, it was mentioned that all the Mesoamerican peoples had a calendar which entailed the meshing of the days of a 260-day 'Almanac Year' with those of the 365-day solar year. A day in one would not meet a day in the other for 52 years; consequently, any date could be placed within a single 52-year cycle by this means. This is the Calendar Round system, but it obviously is not much help when more than 52 years is involved (just as a Maori would not know what revolution occurred in '76, or a Choctaw what happened to an English king in '88), for it would require special knowledge to know in which century the event happened. A more exact way of expressing dates would be a system which counted days elapsed from a definite starting point, such as the founding of Rome or the birth of Christ. This is the role that was fulfilled by the Long Count, confined to the lowland peoples of Mesoamerica and taken to its greatest refinement by the Classic Maya. For reasons unknown to us, the starting date was 13 August 3114 BC (Gregorian), and dates are presented in terms of the numbers of periods of varying length

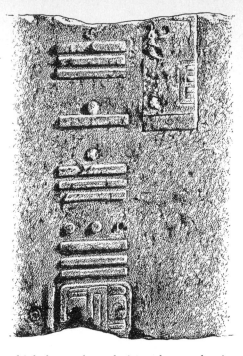

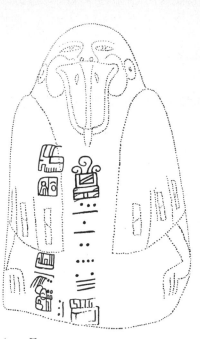

which have elapsed since the mechanism was set in motion. For instance, the largest period was one of 144,000 days, the next of 7,200 days, then 360 days, followed by 20 days and one day. Coefficients were expressed in terms of bar-and-dot numerals, the bars having the value of five and the dots, one. Thus, a bar and two dots stand for 'seven'.

In Stela C, the coefficient accompanying the great first period was missing when the stone was discovered by Matthew Stirling, but he reconstructed it as seven. He read the entire date as (7).16.6.16.18, or 3 September 32 BC in terms of our calendar, raising a storm of protests from Mayanists who felt sure that a monument outside Maya territory could not be this old. Stirling was vindicated in 1969 when a Tres Zapotes farmer accidentally turned up the missing top part of the stela, complete with its coefficient of seven. Another date, this time with a fairly long, unread text, is inscribed on a small jade figure in epi-Olmec style, a duck-billed, winged figure with human features. This is the Tuxtla Statuette, discovered many years ago in the Olmec area, with the Long Count date of 8.6.2.4.17 (14 March AD 162). Since both dates fall in the Late Formative and were found within the Olmec heartland, it is not unlikely that Olmec literati invented the Long Count and perhaps also developed certain astronomical observations with which the Maya are usually credited.

However, the earliest Long Count date of all turned up on a reused slab at the site of Chiapa de Corzo, in the Grijalva Depression of Chiapas, outside the heartland proper. It bears a date which can be reconstructed as (7.16)3.2.13 or 8 December 36 BC, some four years earlier than Stela C. Quite possibly, we have not yet discovered the answer to where, when, and why the Long Count was invented.

48 Lower part of Long Count date on Stela C, Tres Zapotes.

49 The Tuxtla Statuette, with Long Count date and other hieroglyphs. Ht 15 cm.

48

49

The Olmec frontier

Notwithstanding their intellectual and artistic achievements, the Olmec were by no means a peaceful people. Their monuments show that they fought battles with war clubs, and some individuals carry what seems to be a kind of cestus or knuckle-duster. Whether the indubitable Olmec presence in highland Mexico represents actual invasion from the heartland is still under debate. The Olmec of sites like San Lorenzo and La Venta certainly needed substances, often of a prestigious nature, which were unobtainable in their homeland – obsidian, iron-ore for mirrors, serpentine, and (by Middle Formative times) jade – and they probably set up trade networks over much of Mexico to get these items. Thus, according to one hypothesis, the frontier Olmec sites could have been trading stations. Kent Flannery has put forth the idea that the Olmec element in places like the Valley of Oaxaca could have been the result of emulation by less advanced peoples who had trade and perhaps even marriage ties with the Olmec élite. And finally, the occurrence of iconography based on the Olmec pantheon over a wide area of Mesoamerica suggests the possibility of missionary efforts on the part of the heartland Olmec.

Among the sites in central Mexico which have produced Early Formative Olmec objects, principally figurines and ceramics, are Tlatilco and Tlapacoya in the Valley of Mexico, and Las Bocas in Puebla; from the latter have come bowls, bottles, and effigy vases, along with fine, white kaolin Olmec babies and human effigies. Many of these items might have been manufactured at San Lorenzo itself.

Although it is still in the highlands, the state of Morelos, to the south of the Valley of Mexico, is warm and even subtropical, and might well have proved attractive for the Olmec. Chalcatzingo is the most important frontier Olmec site, and lies in the Amatzinac Valley of eastern Morelos. There, three isolated, igneous intrusions rise over 300 m above the valley floor, and must have been considered sacred in ancient times, as they were by the Aztec and even the modern villagers. At the juncture of the talus slope and the sheer rock cliff of the central mountain has been found a series of Olmec
50 bas reliefs carved on boulders. The most elaborate of these depicts a woman holding a ceremonial bar in her arms, seated upon a throne; the scene itself takes place within the open, profile mouth of the Olmec earth monster, as though within a cave, which emits smoke or mist. Above this tableau are three stylized rain clouds, from which fall phallic rain drops. The woman must have been a ruler of Chalcatzingo, and the theme is one of power and fertility.

Other sculptures at Chalcatzingo include a relief showing three Olmec warriors brandishing clubs above an ithyphallic captive, and a scene of two rampant felines, each attacking a human. The Feathered Serpent, one of the most important deities of Mesoamerica, makes an appearance on another boulder, with a man disappearing into its open mouth.

In recent years, David C. Grove and Jorge Angulo have directed a University of Illinois project at Chalcatzingo, which has

50 Relief 1, Chalcatzingo, Morelos. A woman ruler is seated within a cave or stylized monster mouth which gives off smoke or steam, while raindrops fall from clouds above. Olmec culture, Middle Formative period. Ht 3.2 m.

cleared up many of the mysteries posed by Chalcatzingo. The site itself, which consists of platform mounds and terraces below the central mountain, was founded by about 1500 BC, but reached its height during the Middle Formative Cantera phase, from 700 to 500 BC, at which time the carvings were apparently made. They are therefore coeval with the apogee of La Venta, which surely was the center from which Olmec influence emanated to Morelos. The Illinois project discovered a table-top 'altar' with a relief of the earth monster's mouth; a child, probably a human sacrifice, had been buried within the 'altar'. The Chalcatzingo élite received elaborate crypt burials, one being accompanied by a greenstone figure in the purest La Venta style; jade earspools, pendants, and necklaces were also present.

Although this part of Morelos is somewhat arid, the Cantera phase farmers did little irrigation, but planted their crops on artificial terraces. Deer and cottontail were hunted, but the most prominent food animal, as in most Formative sites, was the dog.

Grove, like Flannery, is skeptical about whether a frontier site like Chalcatzingo actually represents an invasion or takeover by Gulf Coast people, and he also favors the idea of Olmec influence coming in through long-distance trade and marriage alliances. In his view, the monuments, many of which depict the Chalcatzingo rulers, have no local antecedents and may well have been carved by artists imported from the heartland to explain the Olmec belief system to the local people.

51 Polychrome painting on the walls of Juxtlahuaca Cave, Guerrero. A bearded ruler with striped tunic, wearing jaguar arm coverings and jaguar leggings, brandishes a trident-like instrument before a black-faced figure cowering on the lower left. Olmec culture, Early or Middle Formative period.

Guerrero is a mountainous, extremely dry state lying south of Morelos, on the way to the Pacific Coast. Many of the most beautiful blue-green Olmec jades have come from this unpromising region, leading Covarrubias to the poorly founded claim that this is where the Olmec must have originated. On the other hand, the still-to-be-detected source of this jade may yet be discovered in Guerrero. Two extraordinary sites show that the Olmec were here, however. Juxtlahuaca Cave had been known for many years; it lies east of the Guerrero capital, Chilpancingo, near the village of Colotlipa, in one of the most arid parts of the state. The cave, whose importance was first revealed by the Princeton art historian Gillett Griffin and by Carlo Gay, a retired Italian businessman, is a deep cavern. Almost a mile in from the entrance is a series of extraordin-51 ary Olmec paintings in polychrome on the cave walls. One of these shows a tall, bearded figure in a red-and-yellow striped tunic, his limbs clad in jaguar pelts and claws; he brandishes a trident-shaped object over a lesser, black-faced figure, probably a captive. Nearby is the undulating form of a red Feathered Serpent, with a panache of green plumes on its head. Deep caves and caverns were traditionally held to be entrances to the Underworld in Mesoamerica, and Juxtlahuaca must have had a connection with secret and chthonic rites celebrated by the frontier Olmec.

Shortly after the Juxtlahuaca paintings were brought to light, David Grove discovered the cave murals of Oxtotitlan, not very far north of Juxtlahuaca. These paintings are in a shallow rockshelter rather than a cavern, and are dominated by a polychrome representation of an Olmec ruler wearing the mask and feathers of a bird representing an owl, the traditional messenger of the lords of the Underworld. He is seated upon an earth-monster throne closely resembling the 'altars' of La Venta. It is extremely difficult to date rock art, but it is possible that Juxtlahuaca may be contemporary with San Lorenzo, and Oxtotitlan with La Venta.

Frontier Olmec sites are found in southeastern Mesoamerica, too, in sites with Olmec carvings and stelae. Perhaps these were left by groups of warrior-traders interested in new sources of precious stones like jade, for Olmec jades have been found in Costa Rica, which may well have had outcrops of this substance, and Costa Rican jades have turned up in Guerrero. Such sites are known for Chiapas; the Pacific coastal plain of Guatemala; and as far southeast as Chalchuapa, El Salvador, around 500 miles from the Olmec homeland, where a boulder is carved with warlike figures in their characteristic style. These groups may have paved the way for missionaries who spread the cult of the were-jaguar and other Olmec gods. But wherever Olmec influence or the Olmec themselves went, so did civilized life.

Early Zapotec civilization

San José Mogote, mentioned in the previous chapter in connection with Early Formative life, remained the most important regional center in the Valley of Oaxaca until the end of the Middle Formative. By that time, it had full-fledged masonry buildings of a public nature; in a corridor connecting two of these, Kent Flannery and Joyce Marcus found a bas-relief threshold stone showing a dead captive with stylized blood flowing from his chest, so placed that anyone entering or leaving the corridor would have to tread on him. Between his legs is a glyphic group possibly representing his name, '1 Motion' in the 260-day ritual calendar. This may be a precursor of the famous *Danzantes* of Monte Albán, and is one of the oldest examples of writing in Mesoamerica.

Toward the close of the Middle Formative, the Zapotec of the Valley were practicing several forms of irrigation. At Hierve el Agua, in the mountains east of the Valley, there has been found an artificially terraced hillside, irrigated by canals coming from permanent springs charged with calcareous waters that have in effect created a fossilized record from their deposits.

Monte Albán is the greatest of all Zapotec sites, and was constructed on a series of eminences about 400 m above the Valley floor, at the close of the Middle Formative, about 500–450 BC, when San José Mogote's fortunes waned. Probably the main reason for its preeminence is its strategic hilltop location near the juncture of the Valley's three arms. It lies in the heart of the region still occupied by the Zapotec peoples; since there is no evidence for any major disruption in central Oaxaca until the beginning of the Post-Classic, about AD 900, archaeologists feel reasonably certain

52 Bas-relief figure of a *Danzante*, Monte Albán, Oaxaca. This is a portrait of a slain enemy, whose name glyph appears in front of his mouth. Monte Albán I culture, Middle to Late Formative period.

that the inhabitants of the site were always speakers of that language.

Most of the constructions that meet the eye at Monte Albán are of the Classic period. However, in the southwestern corner of the site, which is laid out on a north–south axis, excavations have disclosed the Temple of the *Danzantes*, a stone-faced platform contemporary with the first occupation of the site, Monte Albán I. The so-called *Danzantes* (i.e. 'dancers') are bas-relief figures on large stone slabs set into the outside of the platform. Nude men with slightly Olmecoid features (i.e. the down-turned mouth), the *Danzantes* are shown in strange, rubbery postures as though they were swimming or dancing in viscous fluid. Some are represented as old, bearded individuals with toothless gums or with only a single protuberant incisor. About 150 of these strange yet powerful figures are known at Monte Albán, and it might be reasonably asked exactly what their function was, or what they depict. The distorted pose of the limbs, the open mouth and closed eyes indicate that these are corpses, undoubtedly chiefs or kings slain by the earliest rulers of Monte Albán. In many individuals the genitals are clearly delineated, usually the stigma laid on captives in Mesoamerica where nudity was considered scandalous. Furthermore, there are cases of sexual mutilation depicted on some *Danzantes*, blood streaming in flowery patterns from the severed part. Evidence to corroborate such violence comes from one *Danzante*, which is nothing more than a severed head.

53 Bas-relief figure of a bearded *Danzante*, Monte Albán, Oaxaca. Monte Albán I culture, Middle to Late Formative period.

Whereas we have little evidence for writing and the calendar in the Olmec area, there is abundant testimony of both these in Monte Albán I, whence come our first true literary texts in Mexico. These are carved in low relief on the *Danzantes* themselves and on other slabs. Numbers were symbolized by bars and dots, although a finger could substitute for a dot in the numbers 1 and 2. Caso has deduced that the glyphs for the days of the 260-day Almanac Year (based on a permutation of 20 named days with 13 numbers) were in use, as well as those for the 'months' of the solar year. Thus, these ancient people already had the 52-year cycle, the Calendar Round. However, the Long Count was seemingly not in use. A fair number of other hieroglyphs, unaccompanied by numerals, also occur, and these probably were symbols in a script which had both phonetic and ideographic elements, often combined (as in Chinese); some are so placed on the *Danzante* monuments as to attest to their function as proper names, but none can be read.

The pottery of Monte Albán I is known from tombs at this site and in others affiliated with it, such as Monte Negro. It is of a fine gray clay, a characteristic maintained throughout much of the development of Monte Albán. The usual shapes are vases with bridged spouts and bowls with large, hollow tripod supports – typical of the end of the Middle Formative and most of Late Formative. Probably the phase does not begin until about 500 BC and ends about 200 BC. Some of the vessels bear modeled and incised figures like the *Danzantes*, confirming the association.

54 Hieroglyphic inscription on large stone slab, Monte Albán. Monte Albán I culture, Middle to Late Formative period.

55 Fragment of an effigy whistling jar, provenience unknown. The vessel originally consisted of two connected chambers, and when liquid was poured out, air was forced through a whistle in the head. Monte Albán I culture, Middle to Late Formative period.

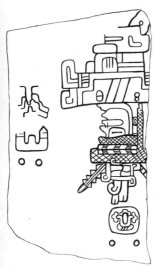

56 Hieroglyphs representing a conquered town, from Building J at Monte Albán. Monte Albán II culture, Late Formative period.

Monte Albán was surely the capital of a burgeoning state during this Late Formative period. Two recent investigators, Richard Blanton and Stephen Kowalewski, give its population as 10,000 to 20,000, and the first Monte Albán palaces seem to appear at this time to meet the administrative needs of the local and Valley-wide citizenry.

The development from the first phase of the site to Monte Albán II, which is terminal Formative and therefore dates from about 200 BC to AD 250, was peaceful and gradual. In the southernmost plaza of the site was erected Building J, a stone-faced construction in the form of a great arrowhead pointing southwest. The peculiar orientation of this building has been examined by the astronomer Anthony Aveni and the architect Horst Hartung, who have pointed out important alignments with the bright star Capella. Within Building J is a complex of dark, narrow chambers which have been roofed over by leaning stone slabs to meet at the apex. The exterior of the building is set with a great many inscribed stone slabs all bearing a very similar text. These Monte Albán II inscriptions generally consist of an upside-down head with closed eyes and elaborate headdress, below a stepped glyph for 'mountain' or 'town'; over this is the name of the place, seemingly given phonetically in rebus fashion (like the 'I saw Aunt Rose' puzzles of youth). Several of these have been identified by Joyce Marcus with known placenames in or near the Valley of Oaxaca given in the post-Conquest Aztec tribute list, such as Cuicatlan, 'Place of Song'. In its most complete form, it is accompanied by the symbols for year, month, and day, and, as Gordon Whittaker has shown, by the indication for the 13-day 'week'. There are also various yet-untranslated glyphs. Such inscriptions were correctly interpreted by Alfonso Caso as records of town conquests, the inverted heads being the defeated kings. It is certain that all are in the Zapotec language.

This obsession with the recording of victories over enemies is one characterizing early civilizations the world over, and the rising Formative states of Mexico were no exception. It speaks for a time when state polities were relatively small and engaged in mutual warfare, when no ruler could extend his sway over a territory large enough to be called an empire.

Dainzú, an important site of Late Formative and Classic date lying some $12\frac{1}{2}$ miles southeast of Oaxaca City, has a large Monte Albán II platform approximately 45 m long; the 1966 investigations of Ignacio Bernal showed that its base was faced with fifty stones carved in low relief, somewhat reminiscent of the *Danzantes*. Most of the figures shown are ballplayers wearing elaborate protective gear, including barred helmets like those borne by medieval knights, knee guards, and gauntlets, and each figure has a small ball in the hand. It is a measure of our ignorance of the early Mesoamerican mind that we are not sure whether these represent the victors or the vanquished!

Izapan civilization

The final culture of the Formative period upon which we will touch is of high significance. This is the civilization centered on the site of Izapa, located in the southeastern part of the state of Chiapas on a tributary stream of the Suchiate River, which divides Mexico from Guatemala. We are here in the broad, Pacific Coast plain, one of the most unbearably hot, but at the same time incredibly fertile, regions of Mexico. Izapa is a very large site, with numbers of earthen mounds faced with river cobbles, all forming a maze of courts and plazas in which the stone monuments are located. There is possibly a ball court, formed by two long, earth embankments. Samples of pottery taken from Izapa show it to have been founded in the Early Formative, and to have reached its height in the Late Formative, persisting into the Proto-Classic period.

The art style as expressed in bas reliefs is highly distinctive. Although obviously derived from the Olmec, it differs from it in its use of large, cluttered, baroque compositions and anecdotal scenes with groups of people. This style appears on stone stelae which often are associated with 'altars' placed in front, the latter crudely carved to represent giant toads, symbols of rain. The principal gods are metamorphoses of the old gods of the Olmec, the upper lip of the deity now tremendously extended to the degree that it resembles the trunk of a tapir. Most scenes on Izapan stelae take place under a sky band in the form of stylized monster teeth, from which may descend a winged figure on a background of swirling clouds. On Stela 1, a 'Long-lipped God' is depicted with feet in the form of reptile heads, walking on water from which he dips fish to be placed in a basketry creel on his back, while on Stela 3, a serpent-footed deity brandishes a club. Most interesting of all is Stela 21, on which a warrior holds the head of a decapitated enemy; in the background, an important person is carried in a sedan chair, the roof of which is embellished with a crouching jaguar.

The real importance of the Izapan civilization is that it is the connecting link in time and space between the earlier Olmec civilization and later Classic Maya. Izapan monuments are found scattered down the Pacific Coast of Guatemala and up into the highlands in the vicinity of Guatemala City. On the other side of the highlands, in the lowland jungle of northern Guatemala, the very earliest Maya monuments appear to be derived from Izapan prototypes. Moreover, not only the stela-and-altar complex, the 'Long-lipped Gods', and the baroque style itself were adopted from the Izapan culture by the Maya, but the priority of Izapa in the very important adoption of the Long Count is quite clear-cut: the most ancient dated Maya monument reads AD 292, while a stela in Izapan style at El Baúl, Guatemala, bears a Long Count date 256 years earlier.

57 Stela 1, Izapa, Chiapas. At the top is a stylized mouth representing the sky. Below, a god with reptile-head feet is dipping fish from the water with a net; he carries a bottle-shaped creel strapped to his back. Izapan style, Late Formative period. Ht 1.93 m.

6
The Classic period

Rise of the great civilizations

By any criteria, the period from about AD 150 to 900 was the most remarkable in the whole development of Mesoamerica. This era of florescence is the Classic, and it is at this time that the peoples of Mexico built civilizations that can bear comparison with those of other parts of the globe. With justification, the Classic is thought of as the Golden Age of Mexico, when the arts and sciences reached their highest refinement, when the seeds that were planted during the Formative reached their fruition.   58

It must not be thought that every part of Mesoamerica entered the Classic stage at the same moment. The Classic span is given in most books as AD 300–900, based upon the period during which the lowland Maya were inscribing Long Count dates on their stone monuments. However, central Mexico began the Classic in the second century AD and possibly even earlier, while far western Mexico never seems to have attained Classic florescence.

By this time, literacy was now pan-Mexican, with the probable exception of the western regions. Although no books have survived from the Classic into our day, we have every reason to believe that most peoples possessed them. Dates were recorded in terms of the 52-year Calendar Round, and in the Gulf Coast lowlands the Long Count was used. What for, if not to write their own history?

From their genesis in the Olmec period the gods of Mexico had finally revealed themselves in all their bewildering variety. There had now crystallized a complete pantheon, one that was shared by all Mexicans, and probably, in somewhat altered form, even by the Maya. The most ubiquitous of these deities were the Rain God, perhaps metamorphosed from one of the Olmec were-jaguars; his consort, the Water Goddess; a creator divinity, viewed as an aged Fire God, or as an old man and an old woman; the Sun God; the Moon Goddess; and the Feathered Serpent, known to the later Nahuas as Quetzalcoatl. The latter was a culture hero, revered for his introduction of learning and the arts, and was considered the very essence of life on this earth.

On the basis of older and now out-dated notions about what the Classic Maya were supposed to be like, it used to be thought that the Classic throughout Mesoamerica was a time of general peace and tranquility, without the obsession with warfare and human sacrifice considered typical of the Post-Classic. That idea is probably a delusion stemming from the fact that we have a

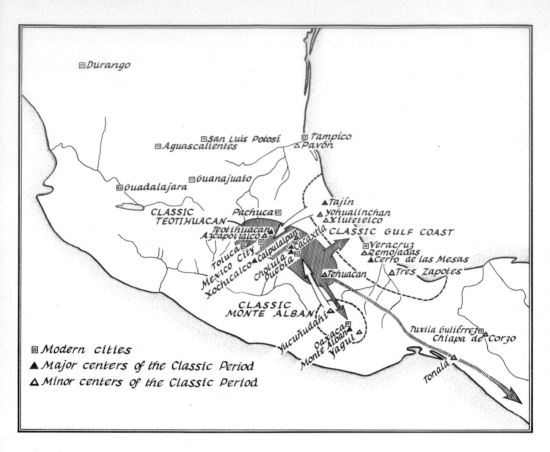

58 Distribution of Classic period sites. The shading indicates the area covered by the Classic Teotihuacan civilization and its extensions in Mexico.

tremendous amount of post-Conquest documentation on the late peoples of Mexico, and none at all on the Classic. It is true that not many fortified sites are known from the Classic, but it should be stressed that all temple clusters and compounds in Mesoamerica were defensible, and that many peoples of this era were careful to place their civic-ceremonial centers on hilltops. In reality, there has never been a people who did not indulge in warfare, including the Classic Maya. In this connection, the sudden spread of the art styles and products of some Classic civilizations has quite justly been interpreted as the result of conquest. Furthermore, in at least one area, the Gulf Coast, human sacrifice was probably as common as it was among the later Aztecs.

There must have been many more people in Mexico during the Classic than formerly. Ruins are everywhere in central and southeastern Mexico, and most of them are Classic. In the Valley of Mexico alone, the monumental survey carried out by William Sanders and his associates has shown that by the end of the Early Classic, there were forty times as many inhabitants of the area than in the Middle Formative.

On the basis of a technology that was essentially Neolithic, for metals were unknown until after AD 900, the Mexicans raised fantastic numbers of buildings, decorated them with beautiful frescoes, produced pottery and figurines in unbelievable quantity, and covered everything with sculptures. Even mass production was introduced, with the invention (or importation from South America) of the clay mold for making figurines and incense burners. Behind this abundance was the same economic theme that had been emphasized by their predecessors: simple farming of maize, beans, and squash, reflected in the continued importance of nature gods in their pantheon. Some authors have claimed that the Classic achievement could only have resulted from utilization of some form of irrigation, but this was of primary importance only in the drier regions of Mexico, such as the Tehuacan Valley and the Valley of Oaxaca.

Very clearly, the Classic florescence saw the intensification of sharp social cleavages throughout Mexico, and the consolidation of élite classes. It has long been assumed that the mode of government was theocratic, with a priestly group exercising temporal power. In lieu of actual documents from the period, there is little for or against this idea to be gained from the archaeological record. At any rate, below the intellectual group which held the political reins was a peasantry which had hardly changed an iota from Formative times. Apart from the post-Conquest introduction of animal husbandry and steel tools, the old village-farming way of life has hardly been altered until today.

How extensive was the sway of each state over surrounding territory may never be known; probably the élite-center type of site held less land and directed fewer people than the great urban state which then had its capital in the Valley of Mexico. In the case of the latter, we may be in the presence of an entity as large as, or larger than, the famous Aztec empire of later days.

The urban civilization of Teotihuacan

True cities of the order of those in the Old World were rare anywhere in the Mesoamerican Classic. Of the few that did exist, the greatest of all was ancient Teotihuacan, the most important site in the whole of Mexico – even Motecuhzoma Xocoyotzin himself made frequent pilgrimages on foot to its ruins during late Aztec times. Memories of its greatness persisted in Nahuatl myths recorded after the Conquest, for it was then thought that the civilization that had begun at Tamoanchan had been transferred to Teotihuacan. There the gods met to decide who was to sacrifice himself so as to become the new, the fifth, sun and bring light again to the world:

> Even though it was night,
> even though it was not day,
> even though there was no light
> they gathered,
> the gods convened
> there in Teotihuacan.[2]

The most humble of them all, Nanahuatzin, the 'Purulent One', cast himself into the flames and became the sun. But the heavenly bodies did not move, so *all* the gods sacrificed themselves for mankind. Finally, government was established there; the lords of Teotihuacan were 'wise men, knowers of occult things, possessors of the traditions'. When they died, pyramids were built above them. The largest of the pyramids, those of the Sun and Moon, were said by tradition to have been built by the giants which existed in those days (thus the legend naïvely says, 'It is not unbelievable that they were made by hand').

The Teotihuacan Valley is actually a side pocket of the Valley of Mexico, comprising about 190 square miles of bottom land lying to the northeast of the Valley proper and surrounded by hills. Of this about one half is suitable for farming. Springs produce copious water which could have been used by the Teotihuacanos for farming, but the evidence for irrigation is not very strong.

A photogrammetric mapping project carried out by René Millon of the University of Rochester gives an idea of the gigantic size of this metropolis. It covers over 9 square miles and was fully urbanized. Teotihuacan was laid out shortly after the time of Christ on a grid plan which is consistently oriented to 15 degrees 25 minutes east of true north, arguing that the planners must have been sophisticated surveyors as well. Various astronomical explanations have been advanced for this alignment, none of them completely

59 Oblique airview of Teotihuacan from the northwest. In the lower left is the Pyramid of the Moon. The Pyramid of the Sun lies at left center. The furthest visible group is the Ciudadela ('Citadel'), connected to the Pyramid of the Moon by the Avenue of the Dead. The city was laid out on a grid plan, and present-day field boundaries correspond roughly to old foundation walls.

convincing. Perhaps the strangest fact regarding this great city plan is that there is absolutely no precedent for it anywhere in the New World.

Teotihuacan's major axis is the Avenue of the Dead, which used to be thought to end at the so-called *Ciudadela* ('Citadel') in the south, a distance of 2 miles from its northern terminus at the Pyramid of the Moon. It is now known that the avenue is *twice* this length, and that it is bisected in front of the Ciudadela by an east–west avenue of equal length, so that the city, like the much later Aztec capital, was laid out in quarters.

The Pyramids of the Sun and of the Moon are explicitly named in old legends, and there is no reason to doubt that they were dedicated to those divinities. The former lies to the east of the Avenue of the Dead and not far from it. Its sides 225 m long and a little over 70 m high, it towers above the surrounding mounds and other ruins. Within it, at the base, are the remains of an earlier pyramid probably as large as the final version. The Pyramid of the Sun was raised in stages during the Tzacualli phase at the site, near the close of the Late Formative. The interior fill is formed entirely of more than 1,175,000 cubic meters of sun-dried brick and rubble. A stone stairway, in part bifurcated, led to a wood-and-thatch temple on its lofty summit. The Pyramid of the Moon was broadly similar, although smaller, and was built during the next phase, Miccaotli, at the beginning of the Classic. Both structures attest the

60 Pyramid of the Sun, Teotihuacan, from the west. Height of pyramid slightly more than 70 m.

60

immense power of the early Teotihuacan hierarchy to call up corvée labor from the villages of the territory over which it ruled. It has been pointed out that in the absence of advanced technology, a powerful state must rely on the work of such 'human ants'.

Discovered by accident in 1971, an extraordinary cave underneath the Pyramid of the Sun throws light on why the Pyramid of the Sun was constructed, and perhaps even on why Teotihuacan itself was built where it was. The cave is actually a natural lava tube enlarged and elaborated in ancient times; it runs 100 m in an easterly direction 6 m beneath the Pyramid, in from the stairway on its main axis, reaching a multi-chambered terminus shaped something like a four-leafed clover. It will be recalled that Aztec tradition placed the creation of the Sun and Moon, and even the present universe, at Teotihuacan. The ancient use of the cave predates the pyramid, and it remained as a cult center after its construction. Unfortunately, official excavations carried out in it were never published, but scholars such as Doris Heyden and Professor Millon note that in pre-Conquest Mexico such caverns were symbolic wombs from which gods like the Sun and the Moon, and the ancestors of mankind, emerged in the mythological past. While there is no spring within the cave, there were channels of U-shaped drains (recalling Olmec prototypes), so that water was probably brought into the cave to flow through them. This immensely holy spot was eventually looted of its contents and sealed off, but the memory of its location may have persisted into Aztec times.

Apart from these early structures, most of Teotihuacan is of Early Classic, and perhaps initial Late Classic, date. By the sixth century AD, it had reached the height of its population, estimated by Professor Millon at a probable figure of 125,000, but possibly reaching 200,000 at its maximum. Teotihuacan was thus the sixth largest city in the world at AD 600.

Classic Teotihuacan architecture is based on a few simple principles. Interiors of adobe bricks or small stones are faced with broken-up volcanic stones set in clay and covered with a smooth coat of lime plaster. The typical architectural motif is that known as *talud-tablero*: a rectangular panel with inset is placed over a sloping wall. Even the tiers of the Pyramid of the Sun are believed to have had this form.

A major finding of the Teotihuacan Mapping Project was that most of the city consisted of modular, residential compounds contained within walls; each is square and about 50 to 60 m on a side. From analysis of excavated artifacts, it seems that these were grouped into something like wards based upon kinship and/or commercial interests. The city was cosmopolitan: in its western part there was an Oaxaca ward, in which Zapotecs carried on their own customs and worshipped their own gods, while on the east there was apparently one made up of merchants from the lowland Veracruz and Maya areas.

The palace compounds were the residences of the lords of the city, such as those uncovered at the zones called by the modern names Xolalpan, Tetitla, Tepantitla, Zacuala, and Atetelco, or the

61 Representation of a temple on a Teotihuacan pottery vessel of the Early Classic period.

magnificent 'Quetzal-Butterfly' Palace near the Pyramid of the Moon. Typical of the palace layout might be Xolalpan, a rectangular complex of about forty-five rooms and seven forecourts; these border four platforms, which are arranged around a central court. The court was depressed below the general ground level and was open to the sky, with a small altar in the center. While windows were lacking, several of the rooms had smaller sunken courts very much like the Roman *atria*, into which light and air were admitted through the roof, supported by surrounding columns. The rainwater in the sunken basins could be drained off when desired. All palaces known were one-storied affairs, with flat roofs built from beams and small sticks and twigs, overlain by earth and rubble. Doorways were rectangular and covered by a cloth.

Something of the sophistication and artistry of the Teotihuacanos can be seen in the magnificent frescoes, usually of gods, which adorn the walls of the palaces. In the porticoes of one of the buildings in the White Patio at Atetelco are depicted processions of jaguars and coyotes, painted in various shades of red, and perhaps

62 Reconstruction of the White Patio, in a palace at Atetelco, Teotihuacan. Early Classic period. Width of floor between the stairways of the two flanking buildings 8.5 m.

63 Prowling coyote from mural painting at Atetelco, Teotihuacan. The painting is done in subtly contrasting values of red. A 'speech scroll' curves from the mouth of the beast, and below the mouth is what is apparently a symbol for the human heart, dripping blood. Early Classic period.

64 (*opposite*) West façade of
the Temple of Quetzalcoatl,
Teotihuacan, transition
between the Late Formative
and Early Classic periods.
On the left, Feathered
Serpents peer out from the
stairway flank; to the right
Serpent heads undulate on
the sloping batters, while
Fire Serpent heads alternate
with Feathered Serpents
within the entablatures.

symbolizing knightly orders. The most famous of the palace murals
are those at Tepantitla, where a large fresco in blue, red, yellow,
and brown covering an entire wall represents the Paradise of the
Rain God, or to use the Nahuatl term, *Tlalocan*. The tableau is
dominated by the deity himself, according to Alfonso Caso. Drips of
water flow from his hands, while in a fanciful landscape little human
figures frolic, sing, and play games. Butterflies and flowering trees
add to the general gaiety of the scene, an evocation of the heaven to
which were translated those who had drowned or otherwise died by
water.

None of these palaces are of sufficient size to have been the
abode of the supreme ruler of the city. The interesting suggestion
has been made by Pedro Armillas that the Ciudadela, a roughly
square enclosure with sides over 640 m long near the center of the
city, was the royal palace itself, since it conforms to the descriptions
of such which we have from the time of the Conquest in the Valley
of Mexico. Within the Ciudadela, on the eastern side of the inner
plaza, is the Temple of Quetzalcoatl, a six-tiered step-pyramid with
typical *talud-tablero* façades, constructed in the Miccaotli phase at
the beginning of the Early Classic period, and partly covered by a
later pyramid. Around the tiers of *talud-tableros*, Feathered Serpents alternate with heads of the Fire Serpent with upturned snout,
bearer of the sun on its daily journey across the heavens. The
background is painted blue, the color of water, and effigy sea shells
are sculpted on its surface. A legend from the Maya highlands
suggests that we have here another version of the first moment of
creation, with an opposed pair of ophidians, one representing life
and greenness and the other heat and the desert regions, cavorting or
conversing in the primal ocean. If this complex really was the royal
palace, then the ruling family may have identified itself with the
center of the universe and the beginning of time.

If palaces alone had been built in ancient Teotihuacan, this
would have been a peculiar sort of city. Some idea of the way more
ordinary people lived is given by the extraordinary ruin discovered
by Linné at the location called Tlamimilolpa, in the eastern part of
the site. This was a crowded cluster of rooms and alleys; although
the ultimate extent of this complex was never determined due to
lack of time, no fewer than 176 rooms, 21 forecourts (*atria*), and 5
courtyards were uncovered. Not all rooms were interconnected, and
apparently groups of these formed private apartments. As yet we do
not know to what degree Tlamimilolpa was typical of the city as a
whole, but there must have been an immense multitude of traders,
artisans, and other non-food producers living in quarters of this
sort. Mexico was to see nothing like this until the Aztecs built their
capital Tenochtitlan.

Many of the gods of the complete Mexican pantheon are already
clearly recognizable at Teotihuacan. Here were worshipped above
all the Rain God and the Feathered Serpent, as well as the Sun
God, the Moon Goddess, and Xipe Totec (Nahuatl for 'Our Lord
the Flayed One'), the last-named being the symbol of the annual
renewal of the vegetation. Particularly common are stone effigy

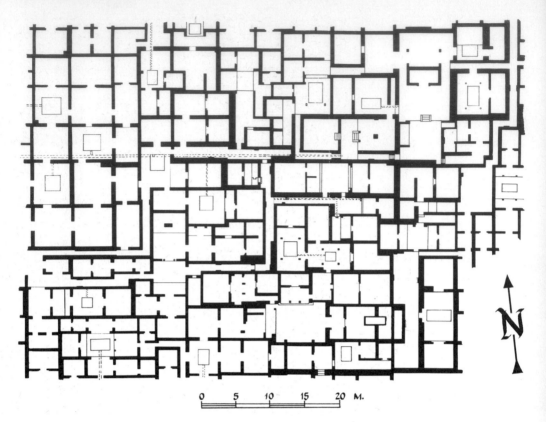

0   5   10   15   20 M.

65 Plan of building complex
found at Tlamimilolpa,
Teotihuacan.

66 Tlaloc, God of Rain, from
a mural painting on a palace
at Zacuala, Teotihuacan.

67 Giant statue of the Water Goddess, Chalchiuhtlicue, from Teotihuacan. Early Classic period. Ht 3 m.

incense burners in the form of the Old Fire God. A colossal statue represents the Water Goddess (in Nahuatl, Chalchiuhtlicue, 'Her Skirt Is of Jade'), but there is an even larger statue, weighing almost 200 metric tons and now in front of the Museum of Anthropology in Mexico City; found in unfinished state on the slopes of Tlaloc Mountain, it is identified in the popular Mexican consciousness with that deity, but its exact identification is unknown. At any rate, it should be noted that almost all the gods venerated in this great urban capital were intimately connected with the well-being of the maize, with their staff of life.

67

Tradition holds that this was a sacred burial ground. Really important tombs have seemingly been discovered only by professional treasure hunters, but underneath the floors of the palaces and apartment buildings have been encountered a number of slab-lined graves. The Teotihuacanos like the later Aztecs favored cremation of the dead, the body first being wrapped in a bundle. Around the remains were placed fine offerings of all sorts, particularly lovely and graceful vases, obsidian artifacts, and perishable things like textiles. Beliefs about the hereafter are recorded in a Nahuatl song:

68 Life-size stone mask in Classic Teotihuacan style. Early Classic period.

And they called it Teotihuacan
because it was the place
where the lords were buried.
Thus they said:
'When we die,
truly we die not,
because we will live, we will rise,
we will continue living, we will awaken.
This will make us happy.'
Thus the dead one was directed,
when he died:
'Awaken, already the sky is rosy,
already sing the flame-colored guans,
the fire-colored swallows,
already the butterflies fly.'
Thus the old ones said
that who has died has become a god,
they said: 'He has been made a god there,'
meaning, 'He has died.'[3]

The Teotihuacan art style as revealed in their frescoes, sculpture, pottery, and other productions is tremendously elegant and refined, as well as highly stylized and ordered. Sculpture is best represented 68 in the austere stone masks, fashioned from greenstone, basalt, jade,

andesite and other materials, each of which once had inlaid eyes of mussel-shells or obsidian, as well as in a few very large-scale pieces such as the Water Goddess.

The hallmark of the Early Classic Teotihuacan culture is the cylindrical pottery vase with three, slab-shaped feet. These vases usually have fitted lids on top with handles in the form of a bird. Other characteristic forms in clay include vessels shaped like flower vases. Decoration on these luxury items, found in graves and far away as trade pieces, commonly is plano-relief, with the cut-away areas painted with vermilion, although the finest have been stuccoed and painted with sacred scenes in the same manner as the wall frescoes. A fine ware known as Thin Orange was apparently manufactured in Puebla, an area under Teotihuacan control, and appears as bowls with annular bases, boxes with lids, or effigies of little dogs.

Other objects of clay include large polychromed incense burners, built up of mold-made details, mold-made figurines of men and gods, and little two-holed *candeleros*, which might have been used to contain blood offered to the gods in an act of self-sacrifice. Clay pellets were carefully shaped for employment as blowgun missiles, and we know from a scene on a vase that this weapon was used in hunting birds.

Obsidian chipping reached new heights of elaboration, with the production of spear and dart points as well as little human effigies of

69 Ceramics from Early Classic burials at Teotihuacan. *a–b*, cylindrical tripods decorated in carved relief technique; *c, florero; d,* 'cream pitcher'; *e*, jar with face of Tlaloc; *f–g, candeleros; h–i*, Thin Orange ware. 1/4.

70

71

70 Fragment of cylindrical tripod vessel with relief design of blowgunner hunting quetzal birds in a cacao tree. From Teotihuacan, Early Classic period. Ht 11.4 cm.

that material. As usual, vast quantities of razor-like blades of obsidian are present. The Teotihuacan state controlled the great deposits of green obsidian near Pachuca, Hidalgo; and the 350 obsidian workshops known to have existed in the city were probably the mercantile basis on which this urban center rested.

Bone needles and bodkins testify to the manufacture of clothing and basketry, and we have the charred remains of cotton cloth with weft pattern, coiled baskets, and twilled sleeping mats or *petates*. Paintings show that men wore a loincloth and/or kilt with sandals, and women the pull-over *huipil* and underskirt.

Although none have survived, books must have been in both ritual and administrative use, for these people had writing. From the few isolated glyphs that have been identified on the pottery and in the frescoes, it is known that they had bar-and-dot numeration and used the 260-day count (Almanac Year).

Cooking was done in kitchen areas within the compounds over clay, three-pronged braziers. Charred vegetal materials and animal bones give some idea of the citizens' diet: they subsisted on a small-cobbed maize, common and runner beans, squashes and pumpkins, husk tomatoes, prickly pear cactus, avocados, and amaranth, along with wild plant foods. The important food animals were deer, dogs, cottontail rabbits and jackrabbits, turkeys, wild ducks and geese, and small fish. Much ink has been spilled over the problem of the agricultural base of Teotihuacan civilization. Professor Sanders is certain that there was a local irrigation system in the Valley itself. On the other hand, there is some evidence of *chinampa* or 'floating garden' cultivation, for relict *chinampa* plots show up on the Millon map of the city, and it is suggestive that the well-known *chinampa* systems in the southern part of the Valley of Mexico, such as the one at Xochimilco, have the same orientation as Teotihuacan itself.

Yet it may be fruitless to look at the Valley of Teotihuacan alone for the secret of the capital's remarkable success, for the city that we have described held sway over most of the central highlands of Mexico during the Early Classic, and perhaps over much of Mesoamerica. Like the later Aztec state, it may have depended as much on long-distance trade and tribute as upon local agricultural production. Teotihuacan influence and probably control in some instances were strong even in regions remote from the capital, such as the Gulf Coast, Oaxaca, and the Maya area. Elegant vases of pure Teotihuacan manufacture are found in the burials of nobles all over Mexico at this time, and the art of the Teotihuacanos dominated the germinating styles of the other high civilizations of Mesoamerica. Six hundred and fifty miles to the southeast, in the highlands of Guatemala on the outskirts of the modern capital of that republic, a little 'city' has been found that is in all respects a miniature copy of Teotihuacan. The tombs of the chiefs of this center, Kaminaljuyú, are full of luxuries from Teotihuacan itself, and it is considered probable that these leaders were invaders from that great Mexican city. A similar situation has been found at that colossus of Maya centers, Tikal, situated in the lowland jungle of northern Guatemala, where an Early Classic monument (Stela 31) shows a jade-bedecked ruler flanked by what seem to be two mercenaries from Teotihuacan.

The question is, and it must be admitted that no definite answer can be given, who were the people of Teotihuacan? Who built this city, and whence did they come? The early Spanish historian Torquemada tells us that the Totonac claimed the honor, and in this light it is true that the earliest Classic Teotihuacan buildings show a certain decorative influence from Veracruz, the Totonac homeland. Some scholars claim an Otomí occupation of the city, others hold for the Popoloca. In view of the strong continuities

71 Chipped obsidian artifacts from Early Classic period at Teotihuacan. *a, c,* and *d,* spear and dart points, 3/8; *b,* human effigy, 3/4.

between Teotihuacan on the one hand and the Toltecs and Aztecs on the other, in both sacred and secular features, the Nahua affinities of this civilization would appear to be the most probable. On this question we are little wiser than were the native peoples, who thought that Teotihuacan had been built by giants or gods.

The city met its end around AD 700 through deliberate destruction and burning by the hand of unknown invaders. It was mainly the heart of the city that suffered the torch, especially the palaces and temples on each side of the Avenue of the Dead, from the Pyramid of the Moon to the Ciudadela. Some internal crisis or long-term political and economic *malaise*, perhaps the disruption of its trade and tribute routes by a new polity such as the rising Xochicalco state, may have resulted in the downfall, and it may be significant that by AD 600, at the close of the Early Classic, almost all Teotihuacan influence over the rest of Mesoamerica ceases. No more do the nobility of other states stock their tombs with the refined products of the great city.

The luxurious palaces of Teotihuacan were now in ruins, and squatters were living within jerry-built walls thrown across the floors, sometimes placing their dead beneath the old rooms like the former inhabitants. This barbaric occupation persisted for about 200 years after the fall of the city, during which a red-on-buff pottery called Coyotlatelco was manufactured, no rival of the beautiful wares of the Teotihuacanos, but in part fashioned on their model. Refugees from the city are thought to have removed to the relatively small center of Atzcapotzalco, west of the great lake, futilely carrying on an epigonal version of their old culture.

A mighty crisis overtook all the Classic civilizations of Mesoamerica during the ninth century AD, the most drastic convulsion being reserved for the Classic Maya, who were forced to abandon most of their centers. In the Teotihuacan Valley, this event took place some two to three centuries earlier, forcing the collapse of civilized life in most of central Mexico before the Late Classic period had really begun elsewhere. Vaillant proposed that the destruction of the surrounding forests necessary for the burning of the lime that went into the building of Teotihuacan resulted in a precocious erosion and desiccation of the region. A related factor might have been the increasing aridity of the climate all over Mexico during the Classic, which apparently was severest in the Valley of Mexico. The whole edifice of the Teotihuacan state may have perished through the ensuing agricultural debacle, opening civilized Mexico to nomadic tribes from the northern frontier.

The Great Pyramid of Cholula

As the present-day traveler leaves the Valley of Mexico and journeys east–southeast across the mountains rimming the basin, he eventually drops down on to the plains of Puebla, the volcanic peaks of Iztaccihuatl and Popocatepetl rising on his right hand. Once on the plain itself, he sees before him shining in the sun the yellow and green tiled domes of a colonial period church which seems to rest

72

on a very large hill. It comes as a shock to realize that this is not a hill at all, but a man-made pyramid, that of Cholula, the largest ancient structure in the New World, and sacred to the god Quetzalcoatl.

The Great Pyramid, which was already in ruins when the Spaniards first arrived, is actually the result of four successive superpositions, all carried out during the Classic period, using mud bricks as fill. The earliest pyramid exhibits strong Teotihuacan influence, with the characteristic *talud-tablero* motif of that site, and is painted with insect-like designs in pure Classic Teotihuacan style. Following the withering of Teotihuacan hegemony over central Mexico, the builders of Cholula worked in an increasingly independent style. For instance, beneath the west face of the Great Pyramid has been uncovered a stone-faced temple substructure with three superimposed *talud-tableros*, the *tableros* embellished with a textile-like mosaic motif; on the south side of the pyramid is a patio with four stone altars, two of which are associated with slab-like stelae carved in relief with the interlaced motifs typical of the Classic Veracruz style.

A 50 m long polychrome mural with life-sized human figures has been discovered at Cholula and is said to be Classic in date; known as 'the Drunkards', the scene is indubitably one of drinking and inebriation, but the liquid imbibed could have been a hallucinogenic potion derived from the powerful mushrooms of ancient Mexico, or even from peyote, rather than alcohol.

In the Early Post-Classic, according to our records, Cholula was taken over by a foreign group known as the Olmeca-Xicallanca, who made it their capital, from which base they controlled the high plateau of Puebla and Tlaxcala. They in turn were overthrown by the Tolteca-Chichimeca – more commonly known as the Toltecs – in AD 1292. Finally, in AD 1359, the kingdom of Huexotzingo, which was in a state of perpetual war with the Aztec, took over this, the holiest site in Mexico. But to all the Post-Classic Mexicans, the Great Pyramid – which in its final form covered an area of 10 hectares and reached a height of 55 m – was one of the wonders of their country. Even when Cortés marched in, memories yet persisted of its traditional dedication to the Feathered Serpent.

72 View from the north of the Pyramid of Cholula, Puebla, crowned with a church of the Colonial period. This great adobe-brick platform, traditionally dedicated to Quetzalcoatl, rises 55 m above the surrounding plain and is the most massive structure of the pre-Columbian New World.

103

The Maya connection: Cacaxtla and Xochicalco

Strange things began happening in central Mexico during and after the disintegration of Teotihuacan's empire in the seventh century AD. One of these was the appearance of foreigners, almost certainly from the Gulf Coast lowlands and the Yucatan Peninsula, towards the end of the Classic period. The interrelationship of the highland Mexicans and the Maya has been established by archaeology, but this was usually the domination by the former of the latter, such as the takeover of Kaminaljuyú by Teotihuacanos. During the Early Classic, there must have been at least one enclave of Maya traders at Teotihuacan, and a fine Maya jade plaque in the British Museum is supposed to have been found at that site. The Maya, with their advanced knowledge of astronomy, probably exerted considerable intellectual and religious influence over the rest of Mesoamerica, and there is some evidence that the dreaded Tezcatlipoca, the great god of war and the royal house in Post-Classic Mexico, was of Maya origin.

There is now reason to believe that there actually were powerful Maya groups in the heart of central Mexico. Cacaxtla is one of a number of hilltop sites in the Puebla-Tlaxcala border area, and lies only $15\frac{1}{2}$ miles north–northeast of Cholula. The early chronicler Diego Muñoz Camargo tells us that it was a 'seat and fortress' of the Olmeca-Xicallanca, whose capital was then Cholula. The name 'Olmeca' (not to be confused with the archaeological Olmec) means 'people of the region of rubber', that is, of the southern Gulf Coast. 'Xicallanca' is another Nahuatl name, referring to 'the people of Xicallanco (or land of calabashes)'. Xicallanco was an important trading town in southern Campeche controlled by the Putun, Maya-speaking seafaring merchants whose commercial interests ranged from the Olmeca country, along the coast of the entire Yucatan Peninsula, as far as the Caribbean shore of Honduras. The late Sir Eric Thompson once referred to them as 'the Phoenicians of the New World'.

In November 1974, looters were discovered working at Cacaxtla; they had uncovered part of an extraordinary mural with colors so fresh that it seemed to have been painted only yesterday. Official excavations have now revealed a palace complex of the eighth and ninth centuries AD, with pilastered rooms arranged around patios and plazas. There is nothing Maya about its flat-roofed architecture, but there are similarities to the coeval palaces of Xochicalco and to the later Tula. The murals appear on the stuccoed walls and jambs of Building A (or Building of the Paintings), and on the *talud* or batter of the substructure of Building B.

The Cacaxtla paintings are thoroughly Maya. More specifically, they are in the style of the ninth-century stelae of Seibal, an important Late Classic center on the Río Pasión in the southern Maya lowlands which was believed by Thompson to have been taken over by the Putun Maya. The North and South Murals flank a doorway, and are associated with unfired clay reliefs showing Maya dignitaries seated on monster-mask thrones. The North

Mural depicts a man with jaguar feet and completely clad in jaguar skin, standing on an elongated jaguar recalling the bearskin rugs of a past generation. He holds an object suggesting the Maya 'ceremonial bar' formed of tied-up spears from which drip blue drops of water; a nearby glyph in Teotihuacan style is to be read as 9 Wind, the calendrical name of Quetzalcoatl, the Feathered Serpent. The jamb has another figure clothed in jaguar pelt.

In the South Mural, the personage wears an eagle costume and has eagle feet, and he also holds a ceremonial bar in his arms; on the nearby jamb, a black-painted figure dances, carrying a large conch shell from which the Maya God N, ruler of the end of the year, emerges.

Both murals suggest some sort of opposition or juxtaposition between Eagles and Jaguars, perhaps symbolic of the knightly orders which we know from Post-Classic Mexico. Such an opposition is vividly depicted on the *talud* of Building B, on which is realistically painted a great battle in progress between jaguar-clad and feathered warriors, any one of whom might be at home on the reliefs of Seibal. There is little doubt that the artist had seen such a conflict, for he depicts such grisly details as a dazed victim, seated on the ground holding his entrails in his hands. The art historian Mary Miller believes that such a battle had actually taken place, perhaps on the swampy plains of southwestern Campeche, but that it had been recast in supernatural terms, in that some of the contestants are improbably given the feet of eagles and jaguars.

73 South Mural at Cacaxtla, Puebla. The figure wears eagle costume and feet, and stands on a Feathered Serpent. Aquatic animals and stylized maize plants frame the scene. Last century of the Late Classic period.

73

74 Another regional center that reached importance with the twilight or disappearance of Teotihuacan's hegemony is Xochicalco, strategically placed atop one of a string of defensively terraced hills in western Morelos. This cosmopolitan entrepôt has been mapped by Kenneth Hirth of the University of Kentucky, who finds it to be the hub of a well-planned network of stone-surfaced causeways with access to the site via well-guarded ramps; this immediately recalls the causeways or *sacbeob* of Classic Maya centers like Tikal. Founded by about AD 700, and possibly extending into the Early Post-Classic, Xochicalco had extensive foreign contacts, especially with the Maya area, Zapotec and Mixtec Oaxaca, and Classic Central Veracruz.

76 Its most striking structure, the Temple of the Feathered Serpent, is a *talud-tablero* platform, but the *talud* element is very high compared with the *tablero*. On the *talud* are sculpted reliefs of great, undulating Feathered Serpents covered with cloud symbols; the folds of the serpents' bodies form a kind of protective shelter to the
75 repeated figure of a man seated tailor-fashion with an elaborate plumed-animal headdress. His name, like that on the North Mural at Cacaxtla, is given Teotihuacan-style as 9 Wind, the birthdate of the god Quetzalcoatl; other dates in the 260-day count are found elsewhere at Xochicalco, and show resemblances to both Teotihuacan and Classic Monte Albán. There is absolutely no prototype for these figures in highland Mexico: they are surely based upon seated rulers carved on Late Classic Maya jade plaques, although the raised edges of the bodies recall reliefs at El Tajín, in the Gulf Coast lowlands.

74 Oblique airview of the fortified hilltop town of Xochicalco, Morelos. This site reached its apogee toward the end of the Late Classic.

75 Detail of personage on the Temple of the Feathered Serpent, Xochicalco, Morelos.

76 Temple of the Feathered Serpent at Xochicalco, Morelos. Figures in Maya style are seated within the serpent's undulations. End of the Late Classic period.

There are numerous caves in the hill on which Xochicalco was built which could have been used for storage purposes by the local population, as Kenneth Hirth suggests. Directly adjacent to the main ceremonial plaza, and not far from the Temple of the Feathered Serpent, is a cave which has been transformed into an underground observatory: a manmade vertical tube leads up to the surface, and on the two days a year when the sun is at its zenith, or directly overhead, a beam of sunlight penetrates the shaft to the cave floor. This may be another case of Maya influence, for zenith passages are known to be important in the ritual calendars of some modern Maya groups, such as the Chorti of eastern Guatemala.

Xochicalco – Maya-influenced and perhaps even Maya-directed – seems to form a kind of bridge between Classic and Post-Classic central Mexico. Xochicalco's ball court, for instance, with its I-shaped layout probably based upon Classic Maya prototypes, has exactly the same dimensions as the ball court at Tula of the Toltecs, which must be several centuries later.

Cerro de las Mesas

Down on the Gulf Coast plain, new civilizations appeared in the Early Classic which in some respects reflect continuity from the old Olmec tradition of the lowlands, as well as intrusive elements ultimately derived from Teotihuacan. The site of Cerro de las Mesas lies in the middle of the former Olmec territory, in south-central Veracruz, approximately 15 miles from the Bay of Alvarado, on a broad band of high land above the swamps of the Río Blanco. The site is the center of an area dotted with earthen mounds. Cerro de las Mesas was occupied from Middle Formative through Late Post-Classic times, but attained its apogee during the Early Classic.

A number of stelae encountered there by Stirling show features recalling both the Olmec and Izapan styles. One side of each monument is generally carved in low relief so as to depict a hieratically posed personage in rich attire, in profile with one leg stiffly outstretched before the other. The Olmec were-jaguar appears in mask-like headdresses and on half-masks which are occasionally worn over the lower face. Two of the monuments record Long Count dates, one being 9.1.12.14.10 (AD 468) and the other 9.4.18.16.8 (AD 533), well within the AD 300–600 span of the Early Classic. Other sculptures include a monstrous figure of a duck-billed human closely resembling the Tuxtla Statuette, which itself was found not very far from Cerro de las Mesas.

Excavations in the site brought to light a fantastically rich cache of carved jade. Altogether there were 782 pieces, buried together at some time in the Early Classic. While some are very much of the period, especially those in the local styles of the Maya highlands and of Oaxaca, a good number are purely Olmec, obviously heirlooms handed down from the ancient civilization that had once controlled this region. Was this cache left by some trafficker in fine jewelry? Does it represent the hoard of some local prince? Or, most plausible of all, is this an offering to the unknown gods of Cerro de las Mesas?

77

77 Stela 6, Cerro de las Mesas, Veracruz. The vertical column on the left records the Long Count date 9.1.12.14.10 (AD 468). The headdress of the richly attired figure on the right is derived from an Olmec prototype.

The Classic Veracruz civilization

A large number of fine stone objects found on the Gulf Coast plain 78
are carved in a very distinct style that has become known as 'Classic Veracruz'. The majority of them are from the northern and central parts of that state, a zone in which are located several great élite centers which shared in the same art tradition. This style can be mistaken for no other in Mexico; on the contrary, its closest affinities seem to lie, for no apparent reason, across the Pacific with the Bronze and Iron Age cultures of China. It is a style in which all subject matter is secondary and bound to a complex ornamental motif, one of linked or intertwined scrolls with raised edges, perhaps the offspring of the cloud scrolls of the Izapan style.

The Classic Veracruz style commonly appears on a complex of enigmatic stone objects, the so-called 'yokes', *palmas*, and *hachas* ('axes' or thin stone heads). Modern research has shown that all three are associated with the ritual ball game, as bas reliefs and figurines depict them being worn in that connection. The 'yokes', 80
which are U-shaped and intricately carved to represent stylized toads covered with convoluted scrolls and human faces, were stone replicas of the heavy protective belts worn by the players. At the front of this ceremonial belt was fitted the *palma*, an elongated 81
sculpture adapted for that purpose; palmas are often effigies of birds like turkeys, or are carved with realistic scenes. The thin stone 82
heads probably were markers placed in the court to score the game. 79

78 (*above left*) Carved slate back for a circular mirror, found in southern Querétaro. The reverse side was the reflecting surface, consisting of a consolidated mass of small pyrite crystals. Classic Veracruz style, Early Classic period. Diameter 15 cm.

79 (*above right*) Thin human head of stone, with headdress in the shape of a crane, designed to fit to the front of a stone 'yoke'. Classic Veracruz style, Late Classic period.

80 (*below left*) Stone 'yoke' in Classic Veracruz style, representing a stylized toad seen from above, covered with scrollwork patterns. Classic period, possibly beginning of Late Classic. Length about 46 cm.

81 (*below right*) *Palma* stone in Classic Veracruz style. The double-strand interlace is highly unusual in this style. Late Classic period. Ht 51 cm.

In its formative phase, the style can best be seen in slate backs for circular mirrors of pyrite mosaic – these are certainly Early Classic in date, as are most of the 'yokes'.

The tribal name 'Totonac' has often been inappropriately applied to these carvings; while it is true that the Totonac now occupy most of the zone in which such remains are found, it may or may not have been they who made them. Archaeologists prefer caution in these matters. Nevertheless, Classic Veracruz influence is very perceptibly present in the beginnings of Classic Teotihuacan, and some are inclined to accept Torquemada's statement that these people built that city. On the other hand, reciprocal influence from the highlands is also present, here on the Gulf Coast.

In accord with the importance of ball court equipment in their art, there are no less than seven ball courts at the most important Classic Veracruz site, El Tajín, an élite center about 5 miles southwest of Papantla, in the rich oil-producing zone of northern Veracruz. The surrounding land is highly fertile for maize, cacao, and vanilla, all of which are still grown. The site derives its name from the belief of the modern Totonac that twelve old men called *Tajín* live in the ruins and are lords of the thunderstorm (and therefore the equivalent of the Rain God).

El Tajín is very extensive, its nucleus covering about 60 hectares, but subsidiary ruins are scattered over several thousand hectares. The site is set among low hills and part of it has been built up with artificial platforms to compensate for the slope. The center was first occupied in the Early Classic, but the peak activity was towards the close of the Late Classic (AD 600–900). Much of El Tajín has never been excavated, but the structures already cleared are striking. The Pyramid of the Niches is a relatively small (only about 18 m high), four-sided structure of wonderful symmetry, faced with carved stone blocks, rising in six tiers to an upper sanctuary. A single stairway climbs to the top, flanked by balustrades embellished with a step-and-fret motif. Around the sides are a number of small square niches, 365 in all, the number of days in the solar year. Inside the pyramid has been discovered a more ancient one, almost a duplicate of the outer.

Other stone buildings at El Tajín are very similar in construction, the step-and-fret design being particularly common. Palace-like buildings with colonnaded doorways were roofed with massive concrete slabs (utilizing marine shell and sand cement mixed with pumice and wood fragments) poured over wooden scaffolds, rather an advanced construction technique for the day. The Building of the Columns is the largest complex at the site; the drums of the columns are carved in reliefs showing winged dancers, Eagle Knights, human sacrifices, and bar-and-dot numerals with day glyphs, testifying to the literacy of this civilization.

Above all, the inhabitants of El Tajín were obsessed with the ball game, human sacrifice, and death, three concepts closely interwoven in the Mexican mind. The courts, which are up to 60 m long, are formed by two facing walls, with stone surfaces either vertical or battered. Magnificent bas reliefs in some of them are witnesses of

82 Stela in Classic Veracruz style, Late Classic period, from Aparicio, Veracruz. Represented is a seated ball player, complete with *palma*; his head has been severed, and seven intertwined snakes sprout from the neck.

83

83 Pyramid of the Niches, El Tajín, Veracruz, looking northwest. Late Classic period. Ht about 18 m.

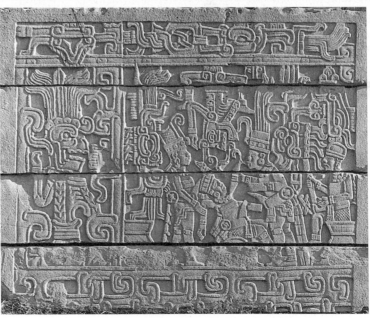

84 Relief panel from the northeast wall of the South Ball Court, El Tajín, Veracruz. The scene depicts the sacrifice of a ball player (the captain of the losing team?). The action takes place in a ball court, and all the figures wear the proper paraphernalia: 'yokes', *palmas*, and knee pads. The Death God rises from a vase on the left to receive the sacrifice. Classic Veracruz style, Late Classic period.

85 Monument on the steps of Structure 5, El Tajín, Veracruz. The Death God emerges from a complex scrollwork design. Classic Veracruz style, Late Classic period.

the drama of the game, for a few scenes show ceremonies involving the players in the court itself, all wearing the appropriate paraphernalia. In one relief, over which the Death God presides, the losing 84 captain is apparently being sacrificed by the victors, who brandish a flint knife over his heart: the game played in the courts of El Tajín was not lightly won or lost. The Death God is ubiquitous at the site, 85 his fleshless skull and skeleton found in both free sculpture and in relief, his bony spine a common architectural motif.

El Tajín probably managed to survive the unsettled transition between the end of the Classic and the beginning of the more militaristic Post-Classic. Its destruction was by fire, and tradition has it that the zone was conquered by the 'Chichimecs', nomadic barbarians from the highlands, at the outset of the thirteenth century AD.

Remojadas potters

An exuberant style in pottery sprang up during the Classic period in a zone of central Veracruz fronting the Gulf of Mexico near the modern port capital of the state. Named Remojadas from the site at which they are most abundant, tens of thousands of hollow clay figurines were fashioned in a naturalistic style from which much ethnographic data can be drawn. The roots of the art reach back to the Late Formative, but most production was during the Late Classic, when Remojadas figurines have close kinship with those of the Classic Maya to the east. Features such as faces were generally cast from clay molds, and a black asphalt paint was used to heighten details or to indicate face paint. The subjects are standing or seated humans, both male and female: curiously infantile boys and girls with laughing faces and filed teeth; ballplayers; lovers or friends in swings; and warriors. The gods are also portrayed: Xipe Totec, as represented by a priest wearing the skin of a flayed captive; the Death God; and probably Quetzalcoatl in his guise as god of wind. The vessels associated with these figurines are generally simple, deep bowls, occasionally with a pleasant polychrome ornamentation.

86 Wheeled pottery toy depicting a deer or a dog, Remojadas style, central Veracruz. The snout and eyes are decorated with asphalt. These amusing toys represent the only application of the principle of the wheel in the New World.

87 Pottery figure of a smiling boy, Remojadas style, central Veracruz. The upper teeth of this individual are characteristically filed. Late Classic period. Ht 52 cm.

88 Pottery figure of an individual wearing the mask of a god, perhaps that of Quetzalcoatl as god of wind. Remojadas style, Late Classic period. Ht 86 cm.

Classic Monte Albán

The civilization of Monte Albán in the Valley of Oaxaca during Classic times was certainly the product of Zapotecan-speaking peoples. The changeover from the Late Formative appears to have been peaceful, with some new elements in the Proto-Classic Monte Albán II coming up from the Maya area as a kind of burial cult: potstands, painted stucco decoration of pottery, and so forth. But Maya influence stops with the commencement of the Classic proper, and a new series of cultural elements holds sway, particularly strong influence being exerted by Teotihuacan. There is no reason to think, however, of any major shift in population or of outside invasion. Furthermore, Oaxaca was sufficiently isolated to avoid some of the troubles visited upon Teotihuacan during the Classic period. Left to themselves to populate their own territory, the Zapotecs built site after site; while in Monte Albán II only 18 or 19 important sites are known, by the close of the Early Classic (Monte Albán III) there were no less than 200 in the Valley of Oaxaca.

The slopes of the hill on which Early Classic Monte Albán stands are covered with hundreds of residential terraces, and Richard Blanton and Stephen Kowalewski, who carried out a detailed survey, estimate a population of 24,000 by Monte Albán III-B times. Most of the Valley's inhabitants were farmers, draining and irrigating the rich bottomlands for their crops, but they must also have farmed the piedmont zone above the Valley.

The Classic site as it now stands was developed around a very large and long plaza. Bigger constructions were raised on rock

89 Building M, northeast corner, Monte Albán, Oaxaca. This structure, a platform–pyramid, is of the Monte Albán III culture Classic period. In the foreground is the Courtyard of the *Danzantes*, of Formative date.

nuclei that remained after the hill was leveled off. Among the buildings of this epoch are stone-faced platforms, fronted by stairways with flanking balustrades. Something like the *talud-tablero* architecture of Teotihuacan is evident, but the panel is modified from its original form. These and other buildings were once stuccoed and beautifully painted. Also present is a magnificent masonry ball court with a ground plan like a capital 'I'; above the sloping playing surfaces are what look like stone grandstands for the spectators.

Subterranean tombs – 170 of them – have been discovered all over the site, some of which were of great magnificence, testimony to the wealth of the lords of Monte Albán. The best are quite elaborate chambers, often with a corbeled vault, and have an antechamber. Fine frescoes were painted on the plastered walls. Tomb 104, in the northern part of the site, is certainly the most spectacular known thus far. Over the façade of the tomb, which is a miniature reproduction of a temple, is a niche containing a pottery urn representing a person wearing the headdress of the Rain God. The door was a single great slab covered with hieroglyphs; within the funerary chamber the skeleton was stretched out on the floor, surrounded by rich offerings including more clay urns. Hurriedly

90

painted while the deceased awaited burial are lovely frescoes which grace the walls, depicting a procession of gods advancing towards the rear of the tomb, interspaced with glyphs. The style of these and other Classic Monte Albán frescoes, down to the smallest details such as treatment of the feather ornamentation, is obviously derivative from Teotihuacan.

Some, at least, of the gods of Monte Albán are shared with other Mexican peoples and can thus be identified. Their divinity finds abundant expression in the numberless pottery urns placed with the dead, often in groups. In these, the use of the mold is eschewed, much of the ornamentation being built up by sharply carved clay strips. Each god is generally shown as seated cross-legged, richly dressed with an elaborate headdress containing the symbol by which he is known. We have in an old dictionary the Zapotec names of some of these deities. The most important members of the pantheon were the Rain God, *Cocijo*; the Maize God, *Pitao Cozobi*, often adorned with actual casts of maize ears; the Feathered Serpent; a Bat God; the Old Fire God; and, possibly, the Water Goddess.

A large group of gods and goddesses are only identified by their calendrical names, and their exact role remains unknown. The writing and calendric system of Classic Monte Albán was fully developed from the Formative base. Although there are no surviving codices, glyphs appear everywhere, both in sculptured relief, on the funerary urns, and painted on walls, at the principal site itself and at other Monte Albán centers. The numeration continues to be in the bar-and-dot system; dates were written with the day signs of

91

90 Part of a painting on the walls of Tomb 104 at Monte Albán, Oaxaca. The Young Maize God appears on the right, holding an incense pouch. Early in Monte Albán III-B culture, *c.* AD 500. Ht of wall 1.6 m.

91 Funerary vessel
representing the Rain God,
from Cuilapan, Valley of
Oaxaca. Monte Albán III-A
culture, Early Classic period.
Ht 69 cm.

the Almanac Year and the 13-day 'week', but also in terms of the
Solar Year. As might be expected, there is some resemblance to
Teotihuacan in these glyphs. Many of the inscriptions are very long;
but, beyond the dates, very little else can yet be deciphered.

While there are no signs of a conflagration, as at Teotihuacan, by
the close of Monte Albán III around AD 700, the capital was largely
abandoned and Monte Albán fell into ruin, as did many other
regional centers in the Valley. Later peoples like the Mixtecs used
the old Zapotec sites as a kind of consecrated ground for their
tombs, some of them as we shall see quite wonderful, perhaps in an
attempt to establish their continuity with the native dynasties which
had ruled here for over a thousand years.

Monte Albán III is succeeded by Monte Albán IV in the Valley, a
Late Classic phase which is yet poorly known, except for the
partially excavated site of Lambityeco in the Valley's southeast arm.
Elite residences and tombs have been discovered there that are in
the Monte Albán tradition, with stone-relief and sculptured-stucco
depictions of an old couple who may be Underworld divinities. But
what is most unusual is the presence of locally made pottery
imitating a ceramic associated with the Putun Maya of Tabasco and
southern Campeche, and even aping the 'slate ware' of Maya sites
like Uxmal and Kabah in the northern Yucatan Peninsula – the
'Maya connection' again!

The Classic downfall

The single most important fact which archaeologists have learned about the Classic period in Mexico is the supremacy of Teotihuacan, its impress being clearly recorded throughout this incredibly varied country. As the urbanized center of Mexico, with high population and tremendous production, its power was imposed through political and cultural means not only in its native highland habitat, but also along the tropical coasts, reaching even into the Maya area. That this was an empire entirely comparable with the Aztec cannot be doubted. In fact, it may have been even bigger than that of Motecuhzoma Xocoyotzin. All other states were partly or entirely dependent upon it for whatever achievements they attained at this time, and any solution of the problem of why the Classic developed at all must be approached through the more central problem that Teotihuacan, without local antecedents, presents to puzzled archaeologists.

When Teotihuacan fell in the seventh century, the unifying force in Mesoamerica was gone, and with it widespread interregional trade. The Late Classic saw increasing fractionalization, each culture moving along its own lines, effectively cut off from the others. In the place of great states and even of an empire, we now have petty kingdoms. Into this power vacuum stepped a people who exhibit all the traits of the Putun Maya. Why should the Maya, until recently considered to have placidly remained within their own boundaries throughout their history, have been intervening in central Mexico's – and perhaps also Oaxaca's – affairs?

To provide even a partial answer, we must examine what was happening to the lowland Maya towards the end of the Classic period, in the ninth century. Beginning shortly before AD 800, the powerful but never unified Maya city-states began to crumble, the sign of the times being their failure to erect dynastic monuments dated in the Long Count system, and by clearcut vandalism and defacement. In this dangerous environment, the Putun (or the Olmeca-Xicallanca, as they were known to the later Aztec), seem to have prospered, as masterful traders and warriors in contact with both the central Mexicans and the declining Maya rulers. We hardly know the true story, but they may have wandered into the Mexican highlands as both merchants and mercenaries, under the leadership of their own *condottieri*, whose exploits may be celebrated by the Cacaxtla murals.

Perhaps agricultural collapse also had something to do with the Classic debacle, or the pressure of outer barbarians to the north, who we know were then knocking at the gates of civilized Mexico. It is as if the pattern of Mexican life, established with the first civilizations of the Formative, had become exhausted. Perhaps the weary farmers of Mexico, and of the Maya area, were no longer willing to build pyramids and palaces for leaders who failed to provide the rains that would guarantee them full harvests.

In short, the country was ripe for revolution as well as conquest from outside, and the two forces probably together produced the different way of life that we see in the Post-Classic period.

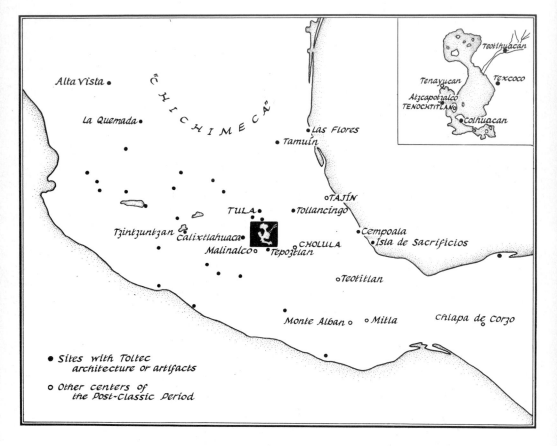

Alta Vista

"CHICHIMECA"

La Quemada

Las Flores
Tamuín

oTAJÍN
TULA   •Tollancingo
Tzintzuntzan   Calixtlahuaca•   Cempoala
Malinalco○ •Tepoztlan   CHOLULA   •Isla de Sacrificios

oTeotitlan

Monte Alban ○   ○Mitla   Chiapa de Corzo

Teotihuacan

Tenayucan   Texcoco
Atzcapotzalco
TENOCHTITLAN○
○Colhuacan

• Sites with Toltec
architecture or artifacts

○ Other centers of
the Post-Classic Period

92 Distribution of Toltec sites and other important centers of the Post-Classic period.
The inset map is the Valley of Mexico.

The Post-Classic period: the Toltec state

A time of troubles

Following in the wake of the widespread disturbances which brought to a close the civilizations of the Classic around the end of the ninth century BC was an entirely new mode of organized life. The salient characteristic of this age, the Post-Classic, was a heightened emphasis on militarism, in fact, a glorification of war in all its aspects. The intellectual hierarchy of the older cultures had now either disappeared or was relegated to inferior status. In its place was an upstart class of tough professional warriors, grouped into military orders which took their names from the animals from which they may have claimed a kind of totemic descent: coyote, jaguar, and eagle. Wars were the rule of the day, those unfortunate enough to be captured destined for sacrifice to gods who were now hungry for the taste of human blood. As a result, for the first time in Mexico there was a widespread need for the construction of strongpoints and the fortification of towns.

92

Throughout Mexico, this was a time which saw a great deal of confusion and movement of peoples, amalgamating to form small, aggressive, conquest states, and splitting up with as much speed as they had risen. Even tribes of distinctly different speech sometimes came together to form a single state – as we know from their annals, for we have entered the realm of history. Naturally, such new conditions are mirrored in Post-Classic art styles, which are thoroughly saturated with the martial psychology of the age. In general they are harder, far more abstract, and less exuberant than those of the Classic period. It is the kind of strong, static art produced by craftsmen guided by Spartan, not Athenian, ideals.

The introduction of metallurgy into Mexico took place towards the end of the Classic period, or at the beginning of the Post-Classic, but had only a slight effect upon the development of native civilization, in contrast to its history in South America and in the Old World. The first cast and beaten metal objects, almost entirely of copper, suddenly appear on the west coast of the Republic, and duplicate in form and technique metal artifacts known from the north coast of Peru and coastal southern Ecuador, making it a certainty that the art was spread north from the Andean area by sea traders plying along the Pacific Coast. Mexican metalwork largely consists of ornaments, particularly small bells cast by the 'lost wax'

93

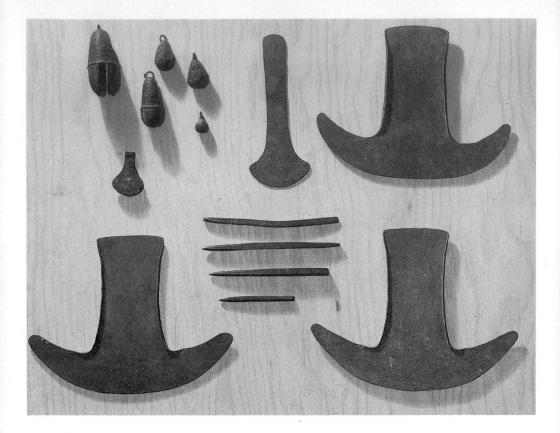

93 Copper tools and ornaments, Post-Classic period. The large 'ax-money' is from Mitla, Oaxaca. The awls are from Lake Chapala in Michoacan, the bells and tweezers from unknown proveniences in Mexico.

method, while implements such as celts or axes are relatively rare and so had little significance in the native tool-kit, which remained on an essentially Neolithic level. In the realm of jewelry, however, the craftsmanship of the Mexican goldsmith reached heights of great artistry, as we shall see.

The northern barbarians

It was not only internal pressure brought by new conquest states that disturbed Mexico. Probably more far-reaching in their long-range effects were the great migrations into Mexico by barbaric tribes inhabiting the wastelands beyond the northern limits of Mesoamerican farming. The Aztecs called all the northerners beyond the pale of civilized life 'Chichimeca', a name meaning something like 'lineage of the dog', not a term of opprobrium since several ruling dynasties in the Valley of Mexico were proud to claim Chichimec ancestry. These barbarians were nomadic hunters who carried their bows and arrows everywhere with them and knew not how to cultivate the land. In the account recorded by Father Sahagún, wildest of all were the 'Teochichimeca', the 'real' Chichimeca, who lived in caves and clothed themselves in animal skins and yucca-fiber sandals, subsisting on wild fruits, roots, and seeds and on the meat of humble animals like the rabbit. Between them and the civilized peoples were the 'Tamime', Chichimeca who had picked up a smattering of the customs and speech of their more advanced neighbors to the south; they wore the cast-off rags of civilization and did a little farming to supplement their wild diet.

Who in fact were the Chichimeca? The inner plateau of northern Mexico is a vast rocky desert bordered on the west and east by the two Sierra Madre ranges. Here lived until recent times primitive tribes like the Uto-Aztecan speaking Zacateca and Tepehuan, the Guachichil of unknown affiliation, and the Pame. These peoples were, then, exactly what the Aztecs meant by 'Teochichimeca'. The heirs of the old 'Desert Culture', forbidden tillage of the soil because of low rainfall, they were mainly collectors of mesquite seeds and hunters of rabbits, which were caught in communal drives. Being perforce semi-nomadic, they traveled in small bands under the leadership of a headman and lived, like the Chichimeca, in either caves or else dome-shaped brush shelters. Lacking from their simple religions were temples, idols, and priests. Most were unfamiliar with pottery or the loom. Easily recognizable here is a mode of existence shared with desert-living Indians as far north as Oregon and one recalling the Archaic background of Mexican civilization.

Dependent upon fluctuations in rainfall, the northern border of Mesoamerica actually wavered back and forth over the centuries, as farmers moved north or were forced back by drought. One long, narrow band of cultivators extended along the moist eastern slopes of the Sierra Madre Occidental almost to the American Southwest; another lay to the west of these mountains, on the coast of western Mexico to the Gulf of California. The peoples of these two strips were not particularly advanced. On the contrary, their position as farmers was rather precarious and they of necessity possessed some of the characteristics of the nomads, just as the frontiersmen of the American West adopted Indian customs as their own. In other words, they were 'semi-Chichimeca' like those Tamime described by Sahagún.

In general, the northerners, like all Desert Culture tribes, were quite peaceful. This was especially so when desert conditions were relatively good; then, increased precipitation brought in farmers from the south and the frontiers marched forward. When, however, the reverse was true, the wild nomads, driven to desperation by drought and starvation, pushed south into regions that were formerly occupied by tillers of the soil, raiding the outposts of civilization. Then, even the part-farmers of the north were pushed back. This would account for the great Chichimec invasions which took place in the Post-Classic period.

Tula and the Toltecs

There have been four unifying forces in the pre-Spanish history of Mexico: the first of these was Olmec, the second Classic Teotihuacan, the third Toltec, and the last Aztec. In their own annals, written down in Spanish letters after the Conquest, the Mexican nobility and intelligentsia looked back in wonder to an almost semi-mythical time when the Toltecs ruled, a people whose very name means 'the artificers'. Of them it was said that 'nothing was too difficult for them, no place with which they dealt was too distant'. From their capital, Tula, they had dominated much of northern and central Mexico in ancient times, as well as parts of the Guatemalan highlands and most of the Yucatan Peninsula. After their downfall, no Mexican or Maya dynasty worth its salt failed to claim descent from these wonderful people.

Like many other Post-Classic states, Toltec society, about which we understand a good deal from later records, was composed of disparate tribal elements which had come together for obscure reasons. One of these, which would appear to have been dominant, was called the Tolteca-Chichimeca. The other group went under the name Nonoalca, and according to some scholars was made up of sculptors and artisans from the old civilized regions of Puebla and the Gulf Coast, brought in to construct the monuments of Tula. The Tolteca-Chichimeca, for their part, were probably the original Nahua-speakers who founded the Toltec state. As their name implies, they were once barbarians, perhaps semi-civilized Chichimeca originating on the fringes of Mesoamerica among the Uto-Aztecans of western Mexico, for although it was said that 'they came from the interior of the plains, among the rocks', their level of culture was substantially higher than that of the 'real' Chichimeca.

Led by their semi-legendary ruler Mixcoatl ('Cloud Serpent', i.e. Milky Way), who was deified as patron of hunting after his death, the Tolteca-Chichimeca by AD 908 had entered civilized Mexico at the southern extension of the Sierra Madre Occidental, passing through what now comprises northern Jalisco and southern Zacatecas. It is no easy matter to reconstruct their history from the contradictory accounts which we have been left, but according to the generally accepted scheme of Jiménez Moreno, Mixcoatl and his people first settled at a place in the Valley of Mexico called Colhuacan. His son and heir was the most famous figure in all Mexican history, a very real person named Topiltzin, born in either AD 935 or 947, and later identified to the confusion of modern scholars with the Feathered Serpent, Quetzalcoatl. This king is described as being of fair skin, with long hair and a black beard.

94

The first event in the rule of Topiltzin Quetzalcoatl was the transfer of the Toltec capital from Colhuacan via Tulancingo to Tula, the ancient Tollan, a name signifying 'Place of the Reeds' but which to the ancients meant something like 'the city'. Some years after its founding, Tula was the scene of a terrible inner strife, for Topiltzin was supposedly a kind of priest-king dedicated to the peaceful cult of the Feathered Serpent, abhorring human sacrifice and performing all sorts of penances. His enemies were devotees of the fierce god Tezcatlipoca ('Smoking Mirror'), the giver and taker away of life, lord of sorcerers, and the patron of the warrior orders, the latter perhaps made discontented by the intellectual pacifism of their king.

As a result of this struggle for power, Topiltzin and his followers were forced to flee the city, perhaps in AD 987. Some of the most beautiful Nahuatl poetry records his unhappy downfall, a defeat laid at the door of Tezcatlipoca himself. Topiltzin and his Toltecs were said to have become slothful, the ruler having even transgressed the rules of continence. Tezcatlipoca undermines the Toltecs by various evil strategems: coming to Topiltzin in the guise of an old man and tricking him into drinking a magic and debilitating potion; then appearing without his loincloth in the marketplace disguised as a seller of green chili peppers, inflaming the ruler's daughter with such a desire for him that her father is forced to take him as son-in-law; next, as a warrior successfully leading a force of dwarfs and hunchbacks which had been given him in vain hope that he would be slain by the enemy; making a puppet dance for the Toltecs, causing them in their curiosity to rush forward and crush themselves to death. Even when they finally killed Tezcatlipoca by stoning, the Toltecs were unable to rid themselves of his now festering, rotted body.

At last, according to legend, Topiltzin Quetzalcoatl leaves his beloved city in exile after burning or burying all his treasures, preceded on his path by birds of precious feather. As Tula disappears from his sight:

> Then he fixes his eyes on Tula and in that moment
>   begins to weep:
> as he weeps sobbing, it is like two torrents of hail
>   trickling down:
> His tears slip down his face;
> his tears drop by drop perforate the stones.[4]

On his way trickster magicians cross his path again and again, trying to make him turn back. At last he reaches the stormy pass between the volcanoes Iztaccihuatl and Popocatepetl, where his jugglers, buffoons, and the pages of his palace freeze to death. He continues on, his gaze directed at the shroud of the snows and eventually arrives at the shore of the Gulf of Mexico. One poem related that there he set himself afire, decked in his quetzal plumage and turquoise mask; as his ashes rose to the sky, every kind of marvelously colored bird wheeled overhead, and the dead king was apotheosized as the Morning Star. Another version of the tale, the one known only too well by Motecuhzoma Xocoyotzin, tells us that he did not perform an act of self-immolation, but rather set off with followers on a raft formed of serpents on a journey to the east, from which he was supposed to return some day.

94 Feathered Serpent from cornice of banquette, Tula, Hidalgo. Toltec culture, Early Post-Classic period.

It is evidence of the historical core within this legend that Maya accounts speak of the arrival from the west, in the year AD 987, of a Mexican conqueror named in their tongue Kukulcan ('Feathered Serpent'), who with his companions subjugated their country. There is also ample evidence in the archaeology of Yucatan for a seaborne Toltec invasion, probably assisted by the Putun Maya, successfully initiating in the late tenth century a Mexican period, with its capital at Chichen Itzá.

With the sanguinary rule of the Tezcatlipoca party now dominant at Tula, the Toltec empire probably reached its greatest expansion, holding sway over most of central Mexico from coast to coast. At the height of its power, Tula is pictured in the poems as a sort of marvelous never-never land, where ears of maize were as big as *mano* stones, and red, yellow, green, blue and many other colors of cotton grew naturally. There were palaces of jade, of gold, a turquoise palace, and one made of blue-green quetzal feathers. The Toltecs were so prosperous that they heated their sweat baths with the small ears of maize. There was nothing that they could not make; wonderful potters, they 'taught the clay to lie'. Truly, they 'put their heart into their work'.

The end of Tula approached with the last ruler, Huemac. Triggered by a disastrous series of droughts, factional conflicts broke out once more, apparently between the Tolteca-Chichimeca and the Nonoalca. In 1156 or 1168 Huemac transferred his capital to Chapultepec, the hill-crowned park in what is now the western part of Mexico City, where he committed suicide. Some Tolteca-Chichimeca hung on at Tula for another fifteen years, finally themselves deserting the city and moving south to the Valley of Mexico and as far as Cholula, subjugating all who lay in their way. Tula was left in ruins, with only memories of its glories. As the Nahuatl poet tells us:

> Everywhere there meet the eye,
> everywhere can be seen the remains of clay vessels,
> of their cups, their figures,
> of their dolls, of their figurines,
> of their bracelets,
> everywhere are their ruins,
> truly the Toltecs once lived there.[5]

The great Toltec diaspora had begun, bands of refugees wandering over highland and lowland Mexico, all claiming Tula as their homeland. Some even penetrated the Guatemala highlands, establishing new dynasties over the Mayas and imposing Mexican customs. In death, as in life, Tula remained the most potent force in Mesoamerica.

Archaeological Tula

It has been the misfortune of modern scholarship that there are not one, but many places named Tula in Mexico – a quite natural circumstance from the meaning of the name. Thus the term was

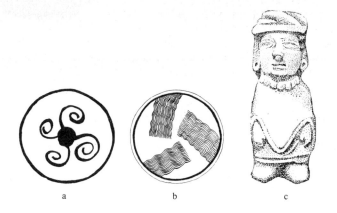

95 Mazapan ceramic artifacts, from Teotihuacan. Pottery of this sort underlies the Toltec culture at Tula. *a–b*, Mazapan red-on-buff bowls, 1/8; *c*, female figurine, 1/2.

indiscriminately applied to great centers like Teotihuacan and Cholula. Given this premise, the glowing descriptions appearing in the native accounts have led many an archaeologist, such as the late George Vaillant, to the erroneous conclusion that the Tula of the Toltecs must have been the admittedly magnificent Teotihuacan. In the late 1930s and 1940s, however, documentary and archaeological researches conclusively proved that the city of Topiltzin and Huemac was the Tula lying to the northwest of the Valley of Mexico, in the state of Hidalgo. More recent archaeological projects undertaken by the Mexican scholar Eduardo Matos Moctezuma and by Professor Richard Diehl of the University of Missouri have given us a deeper knowledge of the Toltec capital.

The real Tula had not only been burned and sacked by its destroyers, but the later Aztecs had thoroughly looted sculptures, friezes, and offerings which were reused in Tenochtitlan and elsewhere. Its reconstruction has been for that reason extremely difficult, and it is little wonder that it now seems unimpressive as one of the major sites of Mesoamerica. Placed in a defensible position on a limestone promontory, Tula is surrounded by steep banks on three sides. Tula's first significant occupation was during the Corral phase (AD 800–900), and is associated with Mazapan pottery, a ware featuring bowls whose interiors are decorated with parallel wavy or straight lines applied by a multiple brush. The Tollan phase (AD 900–1150) marks the apogee of the capital, with the city covering 5.4 square miles, and reaching an estimated population of 30,000–40,000.

95

The main group is of modest area, but mounds extend out for a mile or more. Essentially the center consists of a wide central plaza bordered on the east by the thoroughly despoiled Pyramid C, the largest structure at Tula and as yet unexcavated; on the west by an unexplored ball court; and on the north by Pyramid B and its annexes. On the north side of Pyramid B is a smaller plaza, beyond which is another I-shaped ball court about 37 m long, an exact copy of the prototype at Xochicalco.

96 View from the southeast of Pyramid B at Tula, Hidalgo. This step-pyramid rises in five tiers and has an overall height of 10 m. Toltec culture, Early Post-Classic period.

Pyramid B is the most impressive building at Tula. Built in six successive stages, in its final form this stepped pyramid-platform was fronted by a colonnaded hall, along the back of which banquettes with polychromed bas reliefs of marching warriors were ranged. An ancient visitor would have walked through the colonnade, climbed the stairway and passed through the entrance of the temple, flanked by two stone columns in the form of Feathered Serpents, with their rattles in the air and heads on the ground. The temple itself had two rooms; the roof of the outer one was supported by the heads of four colossal atlantean figures representing warriors carrying an atlatl in one hand and an incense bag in the other – perfect embodiments of Toltec artistic ideals. The rear room had four square pillars, carved on all sides with Toltec warriors adorned with the symbols of the knightly orders. There, in the sanctuary, once stood a stone altar supported by little atlantean figures. Also in the temple and in other parts of the ceremonial precinct were the peculiar sculptures called 'chacmools', reclining personages bearing round dishes or receptacles for human hearts on their bellies; these were probably avatars of the Rain God.

97

98

97 Colossal atlantean figure
of stone, one of the four that
surmount Pyramid B at Tula,
Hidalgo. Each figure is made
of four sections of stone and
represents a warrior carrying
an *atlatl* in one hand and a
pouch for copal incense in
the other. On the chest is
worn the stylized butterfly
emblem of the Toltec. Toltec
culture, Early Post-Classic
period. Ht 4.6 m.

98 Stone 'chacmool' from
Tula, Hidalgo. Reclining
figures of this sort are found
wherever Toltec influence
was felt. This 'chacmool'
wears the Toltec nose-plug
and carries a sacrificial knife
strapped to the upper arm.
Toltec culture, Early Post-
Classic period.

Around the four sides of Pyramid B were bas reliefs symbolizing the warrior orders on which the strength of the empire depended: prowling jaguars and coyotes, and eagles eating hearts, interspersed with strange composite beasts thought to represent Quetzalcoatl.

Adjacent to this pyramid are several very spacious colonnaded halls with sunken courts in their centers. The columns were built up of rubble over wooden cores. Again, low banquettes extend along the walls, which were apparently frescoed. These halls served probably for meetings and ceremonies, rather than as palaces. In fact, two floor plans very closely resembling the palaces of Teotihuacan have been uncovered away from the center of Tula, and these were certainly residences for the rulers of the city.

On the north side of the pyramid and parallel to it is the 40 m long 'Serpent Wall', embellished with painted friezes, the basic motif of which is a serpent eating a human; the head has been reduced to a skull, and the flesh has been partially stripped from the long bones.

The grim Toltec man-at-arms whose features are delineated in stone everywhere at Tula carried the feather-decorated atlatl in the right hand, and a cluster of darts in the left, the Chichimec bow never appearing in the art of civilized Mexico. Protection against enemy darts was provided by a heavy padding of quilted cotton on the left arm and by a round shield strapped to the back. His headgear consisted of a pillbox-shaped hat topped by quetzal plumes and bearing on its front a bird flying downwards. The customary nose ornament was something like a button through the alae, and a goatee often embellished the knight's chin. Over the chest was a highly abstract bird emblem. Either the breechclout (*maxtli*) or the short kilt could be worn, while below leg and ankle bands the feet were shod with backed sandals.

The University of Missouri excavations have brought to light some of the domestic architecture of the Toltecs. Individual houses

99

100

99 (*opposite above*) East side of Pyramid B at Tula, Hidalgo, bas-reliefs of prowling coyotes and felines, alternating with rows of eagles eating hearts and composite monsters. Toltec culture, Early Post-Classic period.

100 (*opposite below*) Bas-relief of eagle eating heart, from east side of Pyramid B at Tula, Hidalgo. Toltec culture, Early Post-Classic period.

101 (*below*) Reconstruction drawing of houses and associated small temple at Tula, Hidalgo. Toltec culture, Early Post-Classic period.

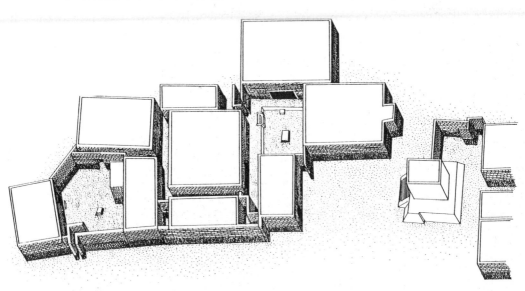

were flat-roofed buildings of square or rectangular plan; these formed complexes of up to five houses, each group separated from others by exterior house walls and courtyard walls. Each such group had a small altar or shrine in the center of the courtyard. The dead were generally buried in a pit beneath the house floor, and accompanied by pots; sacrificial victims formed an exception, these being tossed onto rubbish heaps in abandoned rooms after their bodies had been cannibalized. The general settlement pattern seems to be different from Teotihuacan's, but there is evidence that Tula also had an overall grid plan, organizing these household clusters into wards about 600 m on a side.

Tula is on the margins of Mesoamerica, and it was also marginal for farming, since summer rainfall is insufficient for effective cultivation, and there are winter frosts. Accordingly, food for Tula's population came from the fields irrigated during the rainy season from small canals running from modest check dams.

The Aztec testimony that the Toltecs were mastercraftsmen has not yet been confirmed by archaeology, since excavations have only come up with objects in *tecalli* (Mexican 'onyx', a kind of travertine) as an élite product. But obsidian production was on a huge scale, similar to that at Teotihuacan, and like Teotihuacanos, they controlled the great mines of green obsidian at Pachuca, Hidalgo. In fact, Richard Diehl estimates that more than forty percent of Tula's inhabitants were engaged in production of obsidian cores, blades, and projectile points for internal consumption and export.

The trading, and probably tribute, relationships of Tula within the New World were on an unprecedented scale. The most common foreign trade pottery at the site was the very distinctive Tohil Plumbate ware, one of the very few true glazed ceramics of the pre-Spanish Western Hemisphere, produced in kilns on the Pacific coastal plain near the Mexican–Guatemalan border. Plumbate was probably made to order for the Toltec taste, and one superb vessel was discovered at Tula showing the face of a bearded man (probably Quetzalcoatl) between the jaws of a coyote, all completely covered with small plaques of mother-of-pearl. A storage or cache pit in a room of one house produced five Tohil Plumbate goblets, along with three goblets and a bowl of Papagayo Polychrome, a kind of brightly painted pottery manufactured in quantity at this time in an area extending from eastern Honduras down to northwestern Costa Rica.

In clay one also finds undistinguished moldmade figurines, ladle-like incense burners with long handles, and tobacco pipes with flaring bowls and long stems embellished with undulating snakes. To date, Tula has yielded no metal of any kind, neither copper nor gold, but this need scarcely surprise us, for as yet no fine tombs, where one would expect such treasures, have been located there. On the other hand, many of the ornaments portrayed in stone are painted yellow, a color reserved for gold in the Mexican canon.

There is a singularly secular cast to Tula, for representations of the gods are rare – a state of affairs usually interpreted as the result

102

a   b

102 Plumbate effigy jars from
Teotihuacan and Tula.
Toltec culture. a, bearded
warrior in jaguar helmet; b,
turkey effigy.

of the encroachment of the military over the spiritual power, but it
could well be an artifact of Aztec collecting expeditions. Curiously,
the victorious Tezcatlipoca himself is absent, and the Feathered
Serpent ubiquitous. Quite recognizable are representations of
several deities worshipped also by the Aztecs, such as Centeoci-
huatl, the Maize Goddess; Xochiquetzal, the Goddess of Love; and
Tlahuizcalpantecuhtli, an avatar of Quetzalcoatl as Morning Star.
In line with the claim that human sacrifice was introduced in the last
phase of Tula by the Tezcatlipoca faction, there are several
depictions of the *cuauhxicalli*, the sacred 'eagle vessel' designed to
receive human hearts, as well as a *tzompantli*, the altar decorated
with skulls and crossbones on which the heads of sacrificed captives
were displayed. In fact, the base of an actual *tzompantli* has been
found on the east edge of one ball court; fragments of human skulls
littered its surface. In accordance with Mesoamerican custom,
these were probably trophies from losers in a game that was 'played
for keeps'!

All the evidence points to the death of the city through sudden
and overwhelming cataclysm: the ceremonial halls were burned to
the ground, and the Serpent Wall was toppled over. The fury of the
destruction visited on Tula makes one wonder about the hand that
performed the act. The mere fact that the subsequent reoccupation
of the site was by a people who used so-called 'Aztec' II pottery
does not mean that the vanquishers of the capital were of the same
affiliation. On the contrary the finger of accusation points most
logically once more to the Chichimeca, for Tula was perilously
close to their frontiers. It was just at this time that the barbarians
were again pushing south into cultivated lands. When Xolotl and his
band of Chichimeca passed by Tula on their way to the Valley of
Mexico, they found it already in ruins and spent some days
exploring its shattered walls.

The 'Turquoise Road'

Those hardy pioneers who during Toltec times pushed up north-west along the eastern flanks of the Sierra Madre into Chichimec country, sowing their crops in what had once been barren ground, necessarily were forced to live a frontier life. As a matter of fact, this extension of cultivation into the barbarian zone had begun as far back as the Early Classic period, but it is not until the Post-Classic that one can see any major results, when a series of strongpoints was constructed.

The deep interest of the central Mexicans in the Chichimec zone lying between them and the American Southwest went far beyond the mere search for new lands, however. The site of Alta Vista, near the town of Chalchihuites, Zacatecas, lies astride the Tropic of Cancer, about 390 miles northwest of Tula. It was taken over by Teotihuacan (or Teotihuacan-controlled) people about AD 350, and was exploited all through the Classic for the richness of its local mines, probably, as Professor Diehl thinks, through slave labor. Over 750 mines are known in the area, from which came such rare minerals as malachite, cinnabar, hematite, and rock crystal, which were exported to Teotihuacan for processing into élite artifacts. Alta Vista itself is little more than a ceremonial center with a colonnaded hall on a defensible hill, but it is possible that this architectural trait, along with the *tzompantli* or skull rack, may have provided a Classic prototype for these features at Tula.

At some time in the Classic, turquoise deposits were discovered in New Mexico, in all likelihood by the Pueblo farming cultures that had old roots there. Whether it was they or the Alta Vista people who actually mined the deposits is not known, but turquoise was taken to Alta Vista and worked there into mosaics and similar objects, for export into central Mexico.

103 View from the air of La Quemada, a walled hilltop fortress in Zacatecas, north central Mexico. At the right of the picture is the Hall of Columns. La Quemada was one of the most northern outposts of civilization during Toltec times. Early Post-Classic period.

Alta Vista and its hinterland were abandoned about AD 900, just as the Toltecs were coming to power. Its successor to the control of the New Mexican turquoise sources seems to have been La Quemada, a very large hilltop fortress in the state of Zacatecas, 106 miles to the southwest of Alta Vista. To guard against Chichimec raids, a great stone wall girdles the summit, within which the bulk of the populace (perhaps a Toltec-dominated local tribe) lived, farming the surrounding countryside. Outside the wall, on the lower slopes of the hill, is the ceremonial center of La Quemada: a very odd 10 m high pyramid built up of stone slabs, not truncated and lacking a stairway, along with a colonnaded hall recalling Alta Vista and Tula. On the summit are several platform-pyramids and a complex of walled courts surrounded by rooms.

The two-way nature of the Toltec contact with the Pueblo peoples can be seen at the site of Casas Grandes, Chihuahua, not far south of the border with New Mexico. The florescence of Casas Grandes was coeval with the late Tollan phase at Tula, and with early Aztec. While the population lived in Southwestern-style apartment houses, the Mesoamerican component can be seen in the

104 The Votive Pyramid, La Quemada, Zacatecas. Contrary to the usual Mesoamerican practice, this was not a platform base for a temple. Instead, the walls were originally continued up to a height of nearly 10 m to form the apex of a pyramid. Early Post-Classic period.

presence of platform temple mounds, and I-shaped ball courts, and the cult of the Feathered Serpent. Warehouses filled with rare Southwestern minerals, such as turquoise, were found by Charles DiPeso, the excavator of Casas Grandes. What was traveling north? The Pueblo Indians have a deep ritual need for feathers from tropical birds like parrots and macaws, since these symbolize fertility and the heat of the summer sun. Special pens were discovered at the site in which macaws were kept, apparently brought there by the Toltecs to exchange for the wonderful blue-green turquoise, or perhaps to pay the natives of New Mexico for working the turquoise mines.

It is fairly clear that all these sites were involved in the transmission of Toltec traits into the American Southwest, in particular the colonnaded masonry building and the platform pyramid; the ball court and the game played in it; copper bells; perhaps the idea of masked dancers; and the worship of the Feathered Serpent, which still plays a role in the rituals of people like the Hopi and Zuni. It is also clear that these traits ran along a trading route, a 'Turquoise Road', so to speak, analogous to the famous Silk Road of the Old World that bound civilized and 'barbarian' alike into a single cultural whole.

A similar movement of Toltec traits took place in the southeastern United States at the same time, probably via the people living on the other side of the central plateau, but little is known of the archaeology of that region. In Alabama, Georgia, Tennessee, and Illinois, sites with huge temple mounds and ceremonial plazas, and their associated pottery and other artifacts, show strong Toltec influence. Suffice it is to say here that most of the more spectacular aspects of the late farming cultures of the United States have an ultimately Toltec ancestry.

The Post-Classic period: rival states

Late Zapotec culture at Mitla

Of all peoples of Mexico, the Zapotecs were among the most fortunate, for they had long been undisturbed in their beautiful valley by troublemakers from outside. This state of affairs was ended, however, when Monte Albán was abandoned at the close of the Classic period and a new force was spearheaded by a people infiltrating the Valley of Oaxaca from the mountainous country lying to the northwest. But more of this later.

In the early Post-Classic, a new center of Zapotec civilization sprang up at Mitla, about 25 miles southwest of Oaxaca City. The name is derived from the Nahuatl *Mictlan*, or 'Place of the Dead', but to the Zapotecs it was known as *Lyobaa*, 'Place of Rest'. Not very much is known of the archaeology of Mitla, but it is thought to have been constructed in the Monte Albán V period, corresponding to the Toltec and Aztec eras; it was still in use when the Spaniards arrived.

Mitla is one of the architectural wonders of ancient Mexico – not grandiose, not a mighty city it is true, but of unparalleled beauty. Five groups of palace-like structures are scattered over the site, 105 which is guarded by a fortified stronghold on a nearby hill. A Colonial church is built into one of these palaces and during fiestas native Zapotec ceremonies are still carried out within its precincts, side by side with Christian rites. Most remarkable among these complexes is the Group of the Columns, comprising very long masonry halls arranged on platforms around the four sides of a plaza. Here and elsewhere at Mitla long panels and entire walls are covered with geometric stonework mosaics, the intricate arabesques 106 of which are almost entirely based on the step-and-fret motif, each piece of veneer being set into a red stucco background. From the descriptions handed down from the Colonial period, it is known that the spacious rooms of the palaces had flat roofs supported by huge horizontal beams of wood.

If we can believe the somewhat sensational but highly detailed account of pre-Spanish Mitla given us by Father Burgoa, who visited the district in the seventeenth century, this was once the residence of the High Priest of the Zapotec nation, a man so powerful that even the king bowed to his commands. Mitla's groups of buildings were apparently precincts, one for the holy man himself; one for secondary priests; one for the Zapotec king and his

court when on a visit; and one for the officials and military officers of the king. Priests carried out the ceremonies garbed in white robes and figured chasubles, amid clouds of perfumed copal incense. Hidden from vulgar eyes in an inner chamber of his palace, the High Priest ruled from a throne covered by a jaguar skin; even the king, when in his presence, took a lesser seat. Kept scrupulously clean and covered by mats, the floors were the place of repose for all occupants at night.

Burgoa asserts that gruesome sacrifices took place there continuously: numberless captives had their hearts torn out and offered to the High Priest and the Zapotec gods. Somewhere underneath Mitla was supposed to be a great secret chamber where the Zapotec kings and nobles, as well as heroes killed on the battlefront, were interred, accounting for the name of the site. The exact location of this catacomb is not known, but according to Burgoa the passage leading to it was found in his day and entered by some enterprising Spanish priests, who were soon forced by the horror of the place to scurry out again and seal it up as an abomination against God.

The Mixtecs

'A succession of very small, rather prosperous valleys surrounded by large areas of nearby desert' is how Ignacio Bernal characterizes the homeland of the Mixtec people. This is the mountainous land in western and northern Oaxaca called the Mixteca. Miraculously, there have survived eight pre-Conquest codices which, through the researches of Alfonso Caso, have carried Mixtec history back to a time far beyond the range of any of the annals of other Mexican, non-Maya peoples. However, recent research suggests that Caso was in error in the earliest part of his chronology: instead of starting about AD 700, a date some one and a half centuries later would seem to be correct.

These codices are folding deerskin books written in late pre-Conquest days for the Mixtec nobility. As Jill Furst notes, 'they are concerned with historical events and genealogies, and present records of births, marriages, offspring, and sometimes the deaths of native rulers, and their conflicts to retain their lands and wars to extend their domains.' The one exception is the front, or obverse, of the Vienna Codex, which she has found to be a land document that begins in the mythical 'first time' and establishes the rights of certain lineages to rule specific sites through the approval and sanction of the gods and sacred ancestors.

Designed to be read in *boustrophedon* fashion, that is, zigzag, from top to bottom, the writing on the codices is not truly hieroglyphic but a combination of pictographic and rebus principles, accompanied by dates of the 52-year Calendar Round. Whether this was a Mixtec invention or not, it was also adopted by the Nahua peoples grouped around the Valley of Mexico as their own. Placenames are shown by the rebus-phonetic method, and some have been identified with actual Mixtec centers in Oaxaca.

That the Mixtecs managed to bring under their sway not only all

(Opposite)
105 North façade of the Building of the Columns, Mitla, Oaxaca. Late Post-Classic period. Overall height about 8 m.

106 Portion of inner chamber in Palace II, Mitla, Oaxaca. Late Post-Classic period.

of the Mixteca proper but also most of Zapotec territory by Post-Classic times is a tribute to their statecraft. This was of a simple sort, quite familiar in European history, namely for an aggressive prince to marry into the royal line of a coveted town if he was unable to take it by force; polygamy made this strategy fairly common. Often, if he actually subdued the enemy by force of arms, he would further consolidate his rule by a judicious marriage with a native princess. Extensive intermarriage eventually resulted in the Mixtec aristocracy being one family, under a single dynastic house. As with royalty of Egypt, Hawaii, and Peru, policy considerations led even to brother–sister marriage.

Claiming descent from the Feathered Serpent, they said that their ancestors were born from trees in a certain part of the upper Mixteca. By the beginning of the Post-Classic period, the leading power in the Mixteca was a town called Mountain that Opens; when it was overthrown, its rulers were sacrificed. We now see the establishment of the First Dynasty of Tilantongo, which jointly ruled the valleys with a place called Xipe Bundle, until it too fell.

In the Second Dynasty of Tilantongo, the codices have much to tell about a person named 8 Deer (like most Mexicans, the Mixtecs took one of their names from the day of their birth). Born in AD 1011, his eventful life continued until 1063, during which time the Mixtecs were clearly under powerful Toltec influence. As a boy he accompanied the war parties of his father, the king; he himself soon became a mighty war leader, subduing town after town. In 1045, 8 Deer made a journey to Tula, where he was invested with the Toltec nose button by either the Toltec king himself, a man called 4 Jaguar, or by his chief priest 8 Death; this probably marks his accession to the throne, the ruler of the Toltec capital fulfilling the same function as the pope who crowned the Holy Roman emperor.

We follow in the books the machinations of 8 Deer, as he brings all the rival statelets under his sway: marrying no less than five times, all his wives were princesses of other towns, some of whose families he had subjected to the sacrificial knife. When he was 52

years old, he made the mistake of attacking the native town of the last of his wives, and he himself was captured, suffering the usual fate.

The most mysterious event in his life is the record of his visit to the king of a place called Hill of the Sun, believed by some to be in southern Puebla near Teotitlan del Camino; not only 8 Deer, but the lord of Tula paid homage to this man. Who was he? Was there some empire more powerful than the Toltec about which we know nothing? This is one of the great unsolved puzzles of Mexican archaeology.

By approximately AD 1350 the Mixtecs began to infiltrate even the Valley of Oaxaca by the usual method of state marriage, Mixtec royal brides insisting on bringing their own retinues to the Zapotec court. By the time the Spaniards arrived, practically all Zapotec sites were occupied by the Mixtecs. Of their great wealth and high artistry, for they were the finest goldsmiths and workers in turquoise mosaic in Mexico, the fantastic treasure from Tomb 7 at Monte Albán is eloquent testimony. Here, in an older Monte Albán III-B tomb, the Mixtecs laid the remains of one of their kings and the bodies of his slaughtered servants, some time in the mid-fourteenth century. Accompanying the ruler were magnificent objects of gold, cast in the lost-wax process, and silver; turquoise mosaics; necklaces of rock crystal, amber, jet, and coral; thousands of pearls, one as big as a pigeon's egg; and sections of jaguar bone carved with historic and mythological scenes.

Zaachila, a Valley town still bitterly divided between the descendants of the Zapotecs and the Mixtecs, was a Zapotec capital after the demise of Monte Albán, and had a Zapotec king, but its culture was Mixtec. One of its structures has produced two tombs with a treasure trove of Mixtec-style objects almost equal to those in Tomb 7, including some of the most remarkable polychrome pottery ever discovered in the New World: the ceramic gem in this case is a beautifully painted cup with the three-dimensional figure of a blue hummingbird perched on its rim.

Not only to the south, but as far north as Cholula, Mixtec artistic

107 (*opposite above*) Scenes from the life of the Mixtec king, 8 Deer, from the Codex Nuttall. Right, 8 Deer has his nose pierced for a special ornament in the year AD 1045. Center, 8 Deer goes to war. Left, town 'Curassow Hill' conquered by 8 Deer.

108 (*opposite below*) Gold pendant from Tomb 7, Monte Albán, Oaxaca. The pendant was cast in one piece by the lost-wax process. The uppermost elements represent, from top to bottom, a ball game played between two gods, the solar disk, a stylized butterfly, and the Earth Monster. Mixtec culture, Late Post-Classic period. Length 22 cm.

109 (*above*) Two carved bones from Tomb 7, Monte Albán, Oaxaca. The representations are calendrical and astronomical in meaning. Mixtec culture, Late Post-Classic period. Length about 18 cm.

110

110 Small polychrome, pedestal bowl from Zaachila, Oaxaca. A bright blue hummingbird perches on the rim. Mixtec culture, Late Post-Classic period. Ht of bowl rim 5.4 cm.

influence was felt, resulting in the hybrid Mixteca–Puebla style which produced some of the finest manuscripts, sculpture, pottery, and turquoise mosaics of latter-day Mexico. Although, like several other rival states in Mexico, the Mixtecs were marked down for conquest in its aggressive plans, they were never completely vanquished by the Aztec empire. They united successfully with the Zapotecs against the intruder and thus avoided the fate of so many other once independent nations of Post-Classic Mexico.

The Tarascan kingdom

The Aztecs called the territory of the Tarascans, whom they were never able to conquer, *Michoacan*, meaning 'the place of the masters of fish'. This is a fitting name, for much of Tarascan history centers on Lake Pátzcuaro in western Mexico, which abounds in fish. The Tarascans' own name for themselves and for their unique language is *Purépecha*. While very little field archaeology has yet been carried out in Michoacan, we fortunately have a long and rich ethnohistoric source, the *Relación de Michoacan*, apparently an early Spanish translation of one or more original documents in Tarascan, which gives important details of their past and of their life as it was on the eve of the Spanish Conquest.

In the Late Post-Classic, the Tarascan state was bounded on the south and west by areas under Aztec control, and on the north by the Chichimecs. The people were ethnically mixed, but dominated by the 'pure' Tarascans, who made up about ten percent of the population; many of the groups within their territory were in fact Nahuatl-speakers. The *Relación* tells us of migrations of various tribes into Michoacan, among whom the most important ethnic group called itself 'Chichimec' – probably semi-barbaric speakers of Tarascan, who established themselves on islands in the midst of Lake Pátzcuaro. Their first capital was the town of Pátzcuaro, which was 'founded' about AD 1325 under their hero-chief Taríakuri; from there they imposed their language and rule on the native peoples and on the other tribes.

Eventually, the Tarascans conquered all of present-day Michoacan and established a series of fortified outposts on their frontiers. Ihuátzio, located on the southeastern arm of the lake, became the capital, to be succeeded by Tzintzúntzan, the royal seat of power when the Spaniards arrived on the scene.

At the top of the Tarascan hierarchy was the Kasonsí, the king; he acted as war chief and supreme judge of the nation, and was the ruler of Tzintzúntzan. Under him were the rulers of the two other administrative centers, Ihuátzio and Pátzcuaro, and four boundary princes. The Kasonsí's court was large and attended by a wide variety of officials whose functions give a good idea of the division of labor within the royal household. For instance, there were the heads of various occupational groups, such as the masons, drum-makers, doctors, makers of obsidian knives, anglers, silversmiths, and decorators of cups, along with many other functionaries including the king's zookeeper and the head of his war-spies.

Unlike the Aztec (but like the late pre-Conquest Maya), the Tarascan priesthood was not celibate; the badge of priests was the gourd container for tobacco which was strapped to their backs. At the top of the religious organization was the Supreme High Priest, heading a complex hierarchy with many ranks of priests divided as to function. Tarascan religion was broadly similar to that of the Aztec, but there was a great stress laid upon the worship of fire and of the moon, which seems, like some other Tarascan traits, more South American than Mesoamerican.

There was no formal education for Tarascan boys, who were trained by their fathers for a particular profession or calling, but young women of the aristocracy were educated in a special communal house; these were considered 'wives' of the tribal god Kurikaweri, and usually married off to army officers.

The chronicler of the *Relación* spends many pages on the funeral of the Kasonsí, which was indeed spectacular, but probably not very different from that of any other Mesoamerican ruler of the time. He was borne to his final resting place attended by Tarascan and foreign lords, with elaborate rites and music. Accompanying him in death were seven important women from his palace, such as his 'keeper of the gold and turquoise lip-ornaments', his cook, his wine-bearer, and the 'keeper of his urinal'. Also sacrificed were

III

III View of one of five *yácatas* at Tzintzúntzan, Michoacan, looking north. Tarascan culture, Late Post-Classic period.

forty male attendants, including the doctor who had failed to cure him in his last illness! Quite clearly the Kasonsí's palace was to be replicated for him in the land of the dead.

The ruins of the final Tarascan capital, Tzintzúntzan, rest on a terraced slope above the northeast arm of Lake Pátzcuaro. An enormous rectangular platform 440 m long supports five of the superstructures known as *yácatas*; each *yácata* is a rectangular stepped pyramid joined by a stepped passageway to a round stepped 'pyramid'. The *yácatas* were once entirely faced with finely fitted slabs of volcanic stone that recall the perfection of Inca masonry in South America. Those that have been investigated contained richly stocked burials, and it is probable that their primary function was to contain the tombs of deceased Kasonsís and their retainers.

What little archaeological evidence we have suggests that the Tarascans were extraordinary craftsmen; many luxury objects in collections that are ascribed to the Mixtecs may well come from Michoacan instead, and it has been suggested that the Tarascans may have taken over some of the northern Toltec trade routes after the downfall of Tula. The most astonishing of their productions were paper-thin obsidian earspools and labrets, faced with sheet gold and turquoise inlay, but they were master workers in gold and silver, and in bimetallic objects using both of these precious substances.

The Tarascans deserve further study, particularly through excavations. They were redoubtable warriors, able to turn back the Aztec onslaught, and great artists and architects, with a culture that in several respects recalls the civilizations of the Andes.

The Post-Classic period: the Aztec empire

The beginnings of the Aztec nation were so humble and obscure that their rise to supremacy over most of Mexico in the space of a few hundred years seems almost miraculous. It is somehow inconceivable that the magnificent civilization witnessed and destroyed by the Spaniards could have been created by a people who were not many generations removed from the most abject barbarism, but such was the case. It is only through an understanding of this fact, namely the tribal roots of the Aztec state, that these extraordinary people can really be comprehended.

Peoples and politics in the Valley of Mexico

When any great state collapses, it is inevitable that unless there is another comparable force to take its place, conditions of anarchy will ensue. This is exactly what happened in the Valley of Mexico and surrounding regions in the wake of Tula's destruction in the twelfth century. Refugees from this center of Toltec civilization managed to establish themselves in the southern half of the Valley, particularly at the towns of Colhuacan and Xico, both of which became important citadels transmitting the higher culture of their predecessors to the savage groups who were then streaming into the northern half. Among the latter were the band of Chichimeca under their chief Xolotl, arriving in the Valley by 1244 and settling at Tenayuca; the Acolhua, who founded Coatlinchan around the year 1260; the Otomí at Xaltocan by about 1250; and the powerful Tepanecs, who in 1230 took over the older town of Atzcapotzalco, which it will be remembered was originally founded by Teotihuacan refugees. There is no question that all of these with the exception of the Otomí were speakers of Nahuatl, now the dominant tongue of central Mexico. Thus, by the thirteenth century, all over the Valley there had sprung up a group of modestly sized city-states, those in the north founded by Chichimec upstarts eager to learn from the Toltecs in the south.

It was inevitable that a jockeying for power among these rivals would take place, and it was the northern centers which grew at the expense of the southern. Into this uneasy political situation stepped the last barbaric tribe to arrive in the Valley of Mexico, the Aztecs, the 'people whose face nobody knows'. They said that they came from a place called 'Aztlan' in the west of Mexico, believed by some authorities to be in the state of Nayarit, and had wandered about guided by the image of their tribal god, Huitzilopochtli ('Hummingbird-on-the-left'), who was borne on the shoulders of four priests. Apparently they knew the art of cultivation and wore agave fiber clothing, but had no political leaders higher than clan and tribal chieftains. It is fitting that Huitzilopochtli was a war god and a representative of the sun, for the Aztecs were extremely adept at military matters, and among the best and fiercest warriors ever seen in Mexico. They were also among the most bloodthirsty, for their deity demanded quantities of human hearts extracted from captive warriors, and it was not long before they had a very evil reputation for savagery among their more civilized neighbors.

It was not only their unpleasant habits which failed to endear them, but also the fact that they were outright intruders. All the land in the Valley was already occupied by civilized peoples, who looked with suspicion upon these Aztecs, who were little more than squatters, continually occupying territory that did not belong to them and continually being kicked out. It is a wonder that they were ever tolerated since, women being scarce as among all immigrant groups, they took to raiding other peoples for their wives. The cultivated citizens of Colhuacan finally allowed them to live a degraded existence, working the lands of their masters as serfs, and supplementing their diet with snakes and other vermin. In 1323, however, the Aztecs repaid the kindness of their overlords, who had given their chief a Colhuacan princess as bride, by sacrificing the young lady with the hope that she would become a war goddess. Colhuacan retaliated by expelling these repulsive savages from their territory.

We next see the Aztecs following a hand-to-mouth existence in the marshes of the great lake, or 'Lake of the Moon'. On they wandered, loved by none, until they reached some swampy, unoccupied islands, covered by rushes, near the western shore; it was claimed that there the tribal prophecy, to build a city where an eagle was seen sitting on a cactus, holding a snake in its mouth, was fulfilled. By 1344 or 1345, the tribe was split in two, one group under their chief, Tenoch, founding the southern capital, Tenochtitlan, and the other settling Tlatelolco in the north. Eventually, as the swamps were drained and brought under cultivation, the islands became one, with two cities and two governments, a state of affairs not to last very long.

The year 1367 marks the turning point of the fortunes of the Aztecs, who by this time were calling themselves the *Mexica* or *Tenochca*. It was then that the Aztecs began to serve as mercenaries for the mightiest power on the mainland, the expanding Tepanec kingdom of Atzcapotzalco, ruled by the unusually able Tezozomoc. One after another the city-states of the Valley of Mexico fell to the joint forces of Tezozomoc and his allies; sharing in the resulting loot, the Aztecs were also taken under Tepanec protection, Tezozomoc giving them their first king, Acamapichtli. At the same time, and in fact probably beginning as far back as their serfdom under Colhuacan, the Aztecs were taking on much of the culture that was the heritage of all the nations of the Valley from their Toltec predecessors. Much of this was learned from the mighty Tepanecs themselves, particularly the techniques of statecraft and empire-building so successfully indulged in by Tezozomoc. Already the small island kingdom of the Aztecs was prepared to exercise its strength on the mainland.

The consolidation of Aztec power

The chance came in 1426, when the aged Tezozomoc was succeeded as Tepanec king by his son Maxtlatzin, known to the Aztecs as 'Tyrant Maxtla' and an implacable enemy of the growing power of Tenochtitlan. By crude threats and other pressures, Maxtlatzin attempted to rid himself of the 'Aztec problem'; and in the middle of the crisis, the third Aztec king died. Itzcoatl, 'Obsidian Snake', who assumed the Aztec rulership in 1427, was a man of strong mettle. More important, he had in his chief adviser, the great Tlacaelel, one of the most remarkable men ever produced by the Mexicans. The two of them decided to fight, with the result that by the next year the Tepanecs had been totally crushed and Atzcapotzalco was in ruins. This great battle, forever glorious to the Aztecs, left them the greatest state in Mexico.

In their triumph, the Aztec administration turned to questions of internal polity, especially under Tlacaelel, who remained a kind of grand vizier to the Aztec throne through three reigns, dying in 1475 or 1480. Tlacaelel conceived of and implemented a series of reforms that completely altered Mexican life. The basic reform related to the Aztec conception of themselves and their destiny; for this, it was necessary to rewrite history, and so Tlacaelel did, by having all the books of conquered peoples burned since these would have failed to mention Aztec glories. Under his aegis, the Aztecs acquired a mystic-visionary view of themselves as the chosen people, the true heirs of the Toltec tradition, who would fight wars and gain captives so as to keep the fiery sun moving across the sky.

This sun, represented by the fierce god Huitzilopochtli, needed the hearts of enemy warriors; during the reign of Motecuhzoma Ilhuicamina, 'the Heaven Shooter' (1440–68), Tlacaelel had the so-called 'Flowery War' instituted. Under this, Tenochtitlan entered into a Triple Alliance with the old Acolhua state of Texcoco (on the other side of the lake) and the dummy state of Tlacopan in a permanent struggle against the Nahuatl-speaking states of Tlaxcala and Huexotzingo. The object on both sides was purely to gain captives for sacrifice.

Besides inventing the idea of Aztec 'grandeur', the glorification of the Aztec past, other reforms relating to the political-juridical and economic administrations were also carried out under Tlacaelel. The new system was successfully tested during a disastrous two-year famine which occurred under Motecuhzoma Ilhuicamina, and from which this extraordinary people emerged more confident than ever in their divine mission.

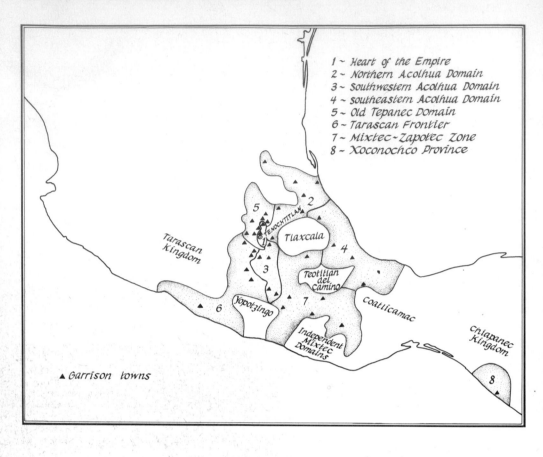

1 ~ Heart of the Empire
2 ~ Northern Acolhua Domain
3 ~ Southwestern Acolhua Domain
4 ~ southeastern Acolhua Domain
5 ~ Old Tepanec Domain
6 ~ Tarascan Frontier
7 ~ Mixtec~Zapotec Zone
8 ~ Xoconochco Province

▲ Garrison towns

112 Extent of the Aztec empire in 1519. The provinces into which the Aztec domains were organized are indicated.

Given these conditions, it is little suprise that the Aztecs soon embarked with their allies on an ambitious program of conquest. The elder Motecuhzoma began the expansion, taking over the Huasteca, much of the land around Mount Orizaba, and rampaging down even into the Mixteca. Axayacatl (1469–81) subdued neighboring Tlatelolco on trumped-up charges and substituted a military government for what had once been an independent administration; he was less successful with the Tarascan kingdom of Michoacan, for these powerful people turned the invaders back. Greatest of all the empire-builders was Ahuitzotl (1486–1502), who succeeded the weak and vacillating Tizoc as sixth king. This mighty warrior conquered lands all the way to the Guatemalan border and brought under Aztec rule most of central Mexico. Probably for the first time since the downfall of Tula, there was in Mexico a single empire as great as, or greater than, that of the Toltecs. Ahuitzotl was a man of great energy; among the projects completed in his reign were the Great Temple of Tenochtitlan, for the dedication of which in 1487 no less than 20,000 captives gained in the 'Flowery War' were sacrificed, and the construction of an aqueduct to bring water from Coyoacan to the island capital.

A more tragic figure in history than his successor, Motecuhzoma Xocoyotzin ('The Younger') (1502–20), would be hard to imagine. It was his misfortune to be a very complex person, not the kind of single-minded militarist that is so well typified by Ahuitzotl. Instead of delighting in war, he was given to meditation in his place of retreat, the 'Black House' – in fact, he was more of a philosopher king, along the lines of Hadrian. Like that Roman emperor, he also maintained a shrine in the capital where all the gods of captured nations were kept, for he was interested in foreign religions. It is certain that the younger Motecuhzoma was deeply imbued with Toltec traditions. This was the cause of his downfall, for when Cortés arrived in 1519, the Aztec emperor was paralyzed by the realization that this strange, bearded foreigner was Quetzalcoatl himself, returned with his Toltecs from the east as the ancient books had said he would, to destroy the Mexican peoples. All his disastrous inaction in the face of the Spanish threat, his willingness to put himself in the hands of Cortés, was brought about by this dedication to the old Toltec philosophy. It was his destiny, foretold by a series of magical portents, to preside over the total destruction of Mexican civilization.

The Aztecs in 1519

Let the soldier Bernal Díaz, who was with Hernán Cortés when the Spaniards first approached the island capital of Tenochtitlan on 8 November 1519, tell us his impressions of his first glimpse of the Aztec citadel:

> During the morning, we arrived at a broad causeway and continued our march towards Iztapalapa, and when we saw so many cities and villages built in the water and other great towns on dry land and that straight and level Causeway going towards Mexico, we were amazed and said that it was like the enchantments they tell of in the legend of Amadis, on account of the great towers and cues and buildings rising from the water, and all built of masonry. And some of our soldiers asked whether the things that we saw were not a dream.[6]

The island was connected to the mainland by three causeways, 'each as broad as a horseman's lance', says Cortés, running north to Tepeyac, west to Tlacopan, and south to Coyoacan. These were broken at intervals by openings through which canoes could pass, and spanned by removable bridges, thus serving a defensive purpose; moreover, access to the city by the enemy was barred by manned gatehouses. Across the western causeway ran a great masonry aqueduct carrying water to Tenochtitlan from the spring at Chapultepec, the flow being 'as thick as a man's body'.

The Spanish conquerors called the Aztec capital another Venice, and they should have known, for many of them had actually been to that place. With a total area of about 20 square miles, the city (meaning by this Tenochtitlan and its satellite Tlatelolco) was laid out on a grid, according to a fragmentary sixteenth-century map of

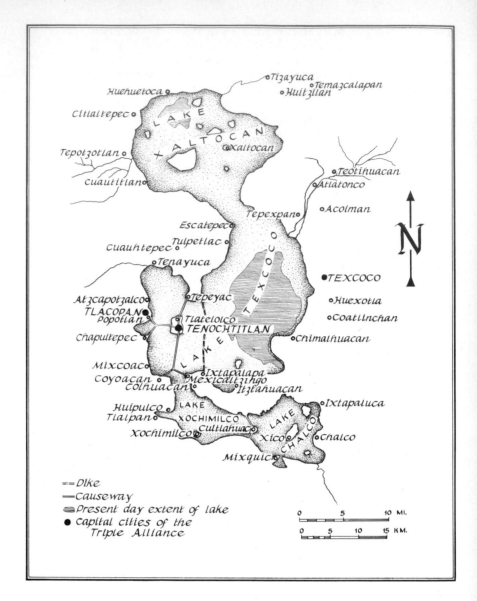

113 The Valley of Mexico in Aztec times.

one section. Running north and south were long canals thronged with canoe traffic and each bordered by a lane; larger canals cut there at angles. Between these watery 'streets' were arranged in regular fashion rectangular plots of land with their houses. In effect, this was a *chinampa* city.

A brief description of *chinampa* cultivation, mentioned in Chapter I, will not be out of place here. The technique is well known for it is still used in the Xochimilco zone to the south of Mexico City, and may have originated with the Teotihuacanos in the Early Classic. It belongs to the general category of 'raised field cultivation', which is widespread in the New World tropics, and was in use among the lowland Classic Maya. The first Aztec settlers on the island constructed canals in their marshy habitat by cutting layers of thick water vegetation from the surface and piling them up like mats to make their plots; from the bottom of the canals they spread mud over these green 'rafts', which were thoroughly anchored by planting willows all around. On this highly fertile plot all sorts of crops were raised by the most careful and loving hand cultivation. This is why Cortés states that half the houses in the capital were built up 'on the lake', and how swampy islands became united. Those houses on newly made *chinampas* were necessarily of light cane and thatch; on drier parts of the island, more substantial dwellings of stone and mortar were possible, some of two stories with flower-filled inner patios and gardens. Communication across the 'streets' was by planks laid over the canals.

The greatest problem faced by the inhabitants was the saltiness of the lake, at least in its eastern part. With no outlet, during floods those nitrous waters inundated and ruined the *chinampas*. To prevent this, the Texcocan poet-king Nezahualcoyotl bountifully constructed a 10 mile long dyke to seal off a spring-fed, freshwater lagoon for Tenochtitlan.

With its willows, green gardens, numerous flowers, and canals bustling with canoes, Tenochtitlan must have been of impressive beauty, as the Nahuatl poem suggests:

> The city is spread out in circles of jade,
> radiating flashes of light like quetzal plumes,
> Beside it the lords are borne in boats:
> over them extends a flowery mist.[7]

It is extraordinarily difficult to estimate the population of the capital in 1519. Many early sources say that there were about 60,000 houses, but none say how many persons there were. The data which we have, however flimsy, suggest that Tenochtitlan (with Tlatelolco) had from 200,000 to 300,000 inhabitants when Cortés marched in, five times the size of the contemporary London of Henry VIII. Quite a number of other cities of central Mexico, such as Texcoco, also had very large populations; all of Mexico between the Isthmus of Tehuantepec and the Chichimec frontier had about 11,000,000 inhabitants, most of whom were under Aztec domination.

At the center of Tenochtitlan, the focal point of all the main 114 highways which led in from the mainland, was the administrative and religious heart of the empire. Surrounded by a 'Snake Wall' was the Sacred Precinct, a paved area dominated by the 40 m high double temple-pyramid, the Temple of Huitzilopochtli and Tlaloc (the Great Temple), its twin stairways reddened with the blood of sacrificed captives. Other temples were dedicated to the cults of Tezcatlipoca and Xipe Totec, the god of springtime. A gruesome reminder of the purpose of the never-ending 'Flowery War' was the *tzompantli*, or skull rack, on which were skewered for public exhibition tens of thousands of human heads. Having hardly more pleasant associations was a very large ball court, in which Mote-

114 The center of Tenochtitlan in 1519, with main streets and canals. *1*, Great Temple of Tlaloc and Huitzilopochtli; *2*, Platform for Stone of Tizoc; *3*, *Tzompantli* (skull rack); *4*, Ball court; *5*, 'Eagle House' of the Sun Temple; *6*, Platform of the 'Eagle House', base for Calendar Stone; *7*, Snake Temple; *8*, Temple of Xipe Totec, God of Spring; *9*, Platform for gladiatorial stone; *10*, Temple of Tezcatlipoca; *11*, Temple of Colhuacan, the former temple of Huitzilopochtli; *12*, Snake Wall, enclosing the sacred precinct; *13*, 'Black House' of the Temple of Coatlicue; *14*, Palace of Motecuhzoma Ilhuicamina (1440–68); *15*, 'House of the Songs'; *16*, Palace of Axayacatl (1469–81); *17*, Royal Aviary; *18*, Palace of Motecuhzoma Xocoyotzin (1502–20).

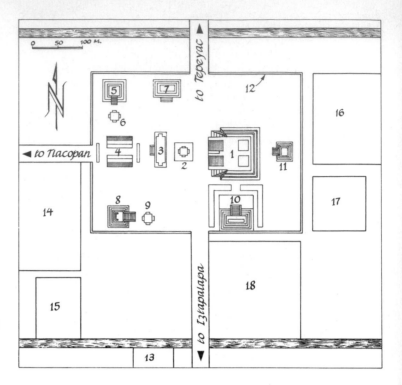

cuhzoma Xocoyotzin played and lost a game to the king of Texcoco on the truth of the latter's prediction that the former's kingdom would fall. The magnificent palaces of the Aztec royal line surrounded the Sacred Precinct.

It has long been known that the ruins of the Great Temple were located a short distance to the northeast of the Cathedral, underneath the buildings of Colonial and modern-day Mexico City. The chance discovery in 1978 of a huge oval monument by workers digging a pit for the installation of power transformers has led directly to the most important Aztec archaeological discoveries of all time. This stone lies directly at the base of the Huitzilopochtli side of the temple, directly in front of one of seven successive rebuildings which the temple had undergone since its foundation. It bears on its upper surface a deep relief of the dismembered body of the goddess Coyolxauhqui, the malevolent sister of Huitzilopochtli, and is one of the masterpieces of the Aztec sculptural art.

115

To understand the significance of this monument, we must recount the legend which lies behind it. Huitzilopochtli, the terrible warrior god of the Sun, was the miraculous result of the impregnation of his widowed mother, Coatlicue ('She of the Serpent Skirt'), by a ball of feathers as she was sweeping one day on Coatepec ('Serpent Mountain'), near Tula. Angered by what they perceived as her dishonor, her 400 sons (the stars of the southern sky), egged on by their sister Coyolxauhqui (almost certainly an avatar of the Moon), decided to kill her; they eventually managed to behead

115 Colossal stone relief of the dismembered goddess Coyolxauhqui, discovered at the foot of an early building of the Great Temple of Tenochtitlan. Aztec culture, Late Post-Classic period. Longest dimension 3.4 m.

Coatlicue, an event commemorated in a magnificent statue of the goddess, a pair of snakes representing the gushing blood issuing from her severed neck. Nevertheless, Huitzilopochtli emerged fully armed from her womb, and slew his sister Coyolxauhqui, hurling her body down from the summit of Coatepec, then pursued and defeated his 400 brothers – surely an astral myth of the defeat by the sun of the moon and the stars.

The importance of the legend, and of its confirmation by the find of the oval monument, is that the Great Temple was known to the Aztecs as 'Coatepec'. This would suggest that there was a representation of Coyolxauhqui in front of each successive Huitzilopochtli pyramid, and such seems to have been the case since two earlier versions of the goddess were found in the right position in older renovations. The spectacular Coyolxauhqui find has led to a massive archaeological project for the Great Temple, with the clearing of the burden of post-Conquest structures.

The Mexican archaeological team under Professor Eduardo Matos Moctezuma has found that the earliest stages of the Great Temple were remarkably crude, as was the associated statuary, in line with the traditional Aztec notion that their ancestors had truly been barbarians when they settled on their island. For example, the murals of the oldest structure were painted not upon plaster, but on mud-daubed walls. All stages of rebuilding were associated with offertory caches, the later ones often containing great deposits of objects from all over the empire, especially Mezcala figurines which the Aztecs had clearly looted from Formative burials in the newly-conquered Guerrero; one remarkably fine Olmec mask even turned up in one offering.

Both in Tenochtitlan and in Tlatelolco proper were great marketplaces, very close to the main temples. The latter market was described by Bernal Díaz in superlative terms; some of the Spanish soldiers who had been in Rome and Constantinople claimed that it was larger than any there. Every product had its own place, the shops being arranged along the streets. So many persons came to buy and sell in the daily markets held there that there were market inspectors appointed by the king to check the honesty of transactions and to regulate prices. As for 'money', cacao beans (which sometimes were counterfeited), cotton cloaks, and transparent quills filled with gold dust served that purpose. Befitting its role as the commercial center of an empire, in the Great Market of Tlatelolco one could buy luxury products of gold, silver, jade, turquoise, or feathers; clothing of all sorts; foods both cooked and unprepared; pottery, the most esteemed being lovely polychrome dishes and cups from Cholula; chocolate and vanilla; carpenter's tools of copper; cane cigarettes, tobacco pipes, and aromatic cigars; and slaves, brought in by dealers from the slave center of Atzcapotzalco and exhibited in wooden cages. The market people had the obligation to furnish war provisions to the state, mainly maize in forms that would not spoil on long marches.

An empire, a tremendous state in place of what had been less than two centuries before but a band of miserable wretches leading a tribal existence – small wonder that the structure of Aztec society was still in a state of transition in 1519. And yet it is utterly false to assert that the Aztecs when first seen by the Spaniards were on the clan level of organization, without any kind of political power greater than that enjoyed by, say, an Iroquois chief. On the other hand, relics of a more simple kind of organization of human affairs certainly persisted in the administration of the empire.

There were four basic social groups in Aztec Mexico. At the top of the ladder were the noblemen or *pilli*, who all belonged to the royal house, 'precious feathers from the wings of past kings', as one source puts it. It was from their ranks that the imperial administrators were drawn; these had the use of lands belonging to their office and also owned private lands.

The vast bulk of the population were commoners, *macehualli*, organized into *calpulli*, or clans, of which there were about twenty in the capital. All members of a *calpulli* (Nahuatl for 'big house') claimed descent from a common ancestor and worked lands which could not be alienated from their group; each family with its plot maintained rights over it as long as it did not lie unused for over two years at a time. As a landholding corporation, each *calpulli* lived in its own ward in the city; Tenochtitlan itself was divided into four great quarters, and every quarter into its constituent *calpulli*, every *calpulli* into *tlaxilacalli*, or streets. Quite obviously, this was an ideal system for administrative control of a large population. The individual *calpulli* had its own temple and some of the more high-ranking of them had schools for the military education of their youth.

At the bottom of the social scale were the bondsmen (*mayeque*), who tilled the estates of the noblemen as serfs; the majority of them would seem to have been the original owners of lands seized from them by Aztec conquest and handed over to be held in severalty by the 'principals'. Another humble group consisted of the *tamime*, porters who hired themselves out to the professional merchants and who may have been semi-civilized Chichimecs from the frontier. Slaves as a group were not important; their membership was drawn from captives and from those who had sold themselves to relieve debts. They were well treated and could not be inherited.

In spite of the presence of clans among the Aztecs, there was nothing in the least bit egalitarian about their society. Everybody was ranked according to their contiguity to the ancestral founders of the *calpulli*, quarter, or nation. As a consequence, there were aristocratic families within the *calpulli* who directed its actions and aristocratic *calpulli* within each quarter. The highest ranking *calpulli* of the greatest quarter in Tenochtitlan was that of the nobility, who claimed descent on the distaff side from Quetzalcoatl; within it, the greatest lineage was that of the royal family. A regular system of tribute offering one third of the products of the soil ensured the maintenance of the clan aristocracies and the nobility, each élite group drawing its support from the units below it.

We see here, then, a society evolved from a more or less primitive organization in which all lands were originally held by the clans and over which there was no higher authority than clan chiefs, into a fully fledged state with the appearance of a privileged class holding authority by virtue of its wealth drawn from private estates worked by a new lower class, the serfs. Given time, the clans would have certainly declined to total insignificance.

Two other groups were also to a certain degree operating outside the old clan system. Warriors distinguished on the field of battle were often given their own lands and relieved from the necessity of supplying tribute. The *pochteca* were the long-distance traders engaged in the obtaining of exotic products for the royal palace. Traveling into foreign territories hundreds of miles from the capital, they gathered military intelligence as well as needed goods for the crown, in special ports of trade. Like the businessmen-spies of modern days, they were often the vanguard for the Aztec takeover of another nation, acting sometimes as *agents-provocateurs*. While organized into their own *calpulli*, with their own god, they could render tribute to the palace in luxury goods rather than the produce of their lands, and grew rich and powerful as a consequence – perhaps the nucleus of a crystallizing merchant class, as some scholars have suggested. But there were powerful sanctions against them flaunting their wealth: as an example, they had to creep into the city at night after a successful trading expedition, lest they arouse the jealousy of the ruler. It is highly doubtful that we have here a middle class in formation.

Motecuhzoma Xocoyotzin, the emperor, was the greatest landowner of all. Among the Aztecs, the king was elected from the royal lineage by a council composed of the nobles, chief priests, and top war officers; at the same time, the four principal lords who were to act as his executive arm were also chosen. On his installation, the new king was taken by the chief priests to pay homage at the temple of the national god, Huitzilopochtli; while he censed the sacred image, the masses of citizens waited expectantly below, in a din caused by the blowing of shell trumpets. After four days of meditation and fasting in the temple, which included prayers and speeches in honor of Tezcatlipoca, the patron deity of the royal house, the king was escorted to his palace. To his coronation banquet came even the kings of distant lands, like the rulers of the Tarascan kingdom, the king of the Totonacs, and great personages from as far as Tehuantepec.

The Aztec emperor was in every sense an absolute ruler, although only in certain domains. His Nahuatl title was *Huei Tlatoani* or 'Great Speaker'; as the researches of Rudolf van Zantwijk have made clear, his function, like that of the 'talking chiefs' among North American tribes, was principally to deal with the external side of the Aztec polity – warfare, tribute, and diplomacy. His counterpart handling the internal affairs of Mexico-Tenochtitlan was the man who held the office of *Cihuacoatl* or 'Female Snake'. The very title celebrates the opposition of male and female principles in the philosophy of dualism so dear to the Aztecs. This man acted as a kind of grand vizier, and was always a close relative of the *Huei Tlatoani*; the most famous *Cihuacoatl* of all was the great Tlacaelel, who transformed the Aztec realm from a kingdom into an empire.

The descriptions of the Spaniards make it clear that the *Huei Tlatoani* was semi-divine. Even great lords who entered into his presence approached in plain garments, heads bowed, without looking on his face. Everywhere he went, he was borne on the shoulders of noblemen in a litter covered with precious feathers. If he walked, nobles swept the way and covered the ground with cloths so that his feet would not touch the ground. When Motecuhzoma ate, he was shielded from onlookers by a gilt screen. No less than several hundred dishes were offered at each meal for his choosing by young maidens; during his repast he was entertained by buffoons, dwarfs, jugglers, and tumblers.

Motecuhzoma's gardens and pleasure palaces amazed the Spaniards. The royal aviary had ten large rooms with pools of salt and fresh water, housing birds of both lake and sea, above which were galleries bordered by hanging gardens for the imperial promenade. Another building was the royal zoo, staffed by trained veterinarians, in which were exhibited in cages animals from all parts of his realm – jaguars from the lowlands, pumas from the mountains, foxes, and so forth, making an unearthly clamor with their roars and howls. Carefully tended by servants, many kinds of deformed persons and monstrosities inhabited his private sideshow, each with his own room.

Less frivolous activities of the royal household included separate courts of justice for noblemen (and warriors) and for commoners; the overseeing by stewards of the palace storehouse; the maintenance of the state arsenal, officers' quarters, and the military academy; and the management of the empire-wide tribute system.

All these state functions, and the Aztec economy itself, ultimately rested on the agricultural base of the Mexican peoples – the farming of maize, beans, squash, tomatoes, amaranth, chía, and many other cultigens. Thousands of canoes daily crowded the great lake, bearing these products to the capital either as direct tribute or as merchandise to be traded for craft items and other necessities in the marketplaces. A tremendous surplus for the use of the city was extracted from the rich *chinampas* fringing the shallow lake and from irrigated fields near by.

But the main goal of the Aztec state was war. Every ablebodied man was expected to bear arms, even the priests and the merchants, the latter fighting in their own units while ostensibly on trading expeditions. To the Aztecs, there was no activity more glorious than to furnish captives or to die oneself for Huitzilopochtli:

> The battlefield is the place:
> where one toasts the divine liquor in war,
> where are stained red the divine eagles,
> where the jaguars howl,
> where all kinds of precious stones rain from ornaments,
> where wave headdresses rich with fine plumes,
> where princes are smashed to bits.[8]

In the rich imagery of Nahuatl song, the blood-stained battlefield was described as an immense plain covered by flowers, and lucky he who perished on it:

> There is nothing like death in war,
> nothing like the flowery death
> so precious to Him who gives life:
> far off I see it: my heart yearns for it![9]

Aztec weapons were the terrible sword-club, with side grooves set with razor-sharp obsidian blades; spears, the heads of which were also set with blades; and barbed and fletched darts hurled from the atlatl. The Aztec warrior was gorgeously arrayed in costumes of jaguar skins or suits covered with eagle feathers, symbolizing the knightly orders; for defence he was sometimes clad in a quilted cotton tunic and always carried a round shield, often magnificently decorated with colored designs in feathers. Acting as mercenaries, fierce Otomí tribesmen accompanied the army as bowmen.

War strategy included the gathering of intelligence and compilation of maps. On the field of battle, the ranks of the army were arranged by generals. Attacks were spearheaded by an élite corps of veteran warriors, followed by the bulk of the army, to the sound of shell trumpets blown by priests. The idea was not only to destroy the enemy town but also to isolate and capture as many of the enemy as possible for transport to the rear and eventual sacrifice in the capital.

116   Nations which had fallen to Aztec arms and those of their allies in
the Triple Alliance were speedily organized as tribute-rendering
provinces of the empire. Military governors in Aztec garrisons
ensured that such tribute, which was very heavy indeed, was paid
promptly and on fixed dates. It is fortunate that the tribute list in
Motecuhzoma's state archives has survived in the form of copies,
for the Spaniards were also interested in what they could extract
from the old Aztec provinces. Incredible as it may seem, each year
Tenochtitlan received from all parts of the empire 7,000 tons of
maize and 4,000 tons each of beans, chía seed, and grain amaranth,
and no less than 2,000,000 cotton cloaks, as well as war costumes,
shields, feather headdresses, and luxury products like amber
unobtainable in the central highlands. Certainly some of this loot,
especially the cloaks, was farmed out by the royal treasury to the
pochteca as barter goods to carry to distant ports of trade. But a good
deal of the tribute acted as the main financial support of the state
edifice, since in an essentially moneyless economy state servants
had to be paid in goods and land, and artisans had to receive
something for the fine products which they supplied to the palace.

Aztec mythology and religious organization are so incredibly
complex that little justice can be given them in the space of this
chapter. The data that we have from the early sources, particularly
from the pictorial books and from Fray Bernadino de Sahagún, are
the most complete in this respect than for any other Mesoamerican
people.

The Aztec concept of the supernatural world was a result of the
reconciliation by mystic intellectuals of the tribal gods of their own
people to the far richer cosmogony of the older civilizations of
Mexico, welding both into a single great system. The bewildering
multiplicity of Mexican gods were to these thinkers but embodiments of one cosmic principle of duality: the unity of opposites, as
personified in the great bisexual creator deity, Ometeotl or 'Dual
Divinity'. In Aztec philosophy, this was the *only* reality, all else being
illusion. Ometeotl presided over a layered universe, dwelling in the
thirteenth and uppermost heaven, while various celestial phe-
nomena such as the sun, moon, stars, comets, and winds existed in
lower heavens. Beneath the surface of the earth were nine stratified
underworlds, through which the souls of the dead had to pass in a
perilous journey until reaching extinction in the deepest level,
Mictlan Opochcalocan, 'The Region of the Dead, Where the
Streets Are on the Left'. This was presided over by another dual
divinity, the dread 'Lord and Lady of the Dead', the infernal
counterpart of Ometeotl.

Out of the sexual opposition embodied in Ometeotl were born
the four Tezcatlipocas. Like all the Mesoamericans and many other
American Indian groups as well, the Aztecs thought of the surface
of our world in terms of the four cardinal directions, each of which
was assigned a specific color and a specific tree on the upper
branches of which perched a distinctive bird. Where the central axis
passed through the earth was the Old Fire God, an avatar of
Ometeotl since his epithet was 'Mother of the Gods, Father of the

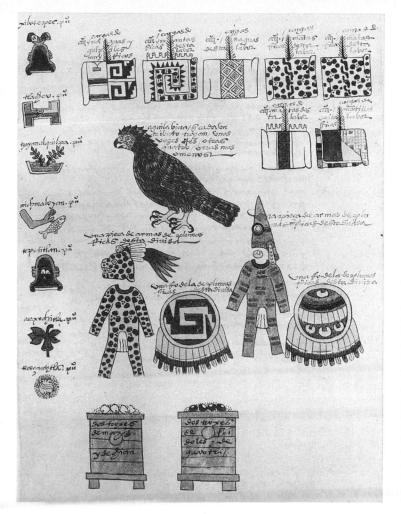

116 Page from the Codex Mendocino, a post-Conquest copy of an Aztec original. This is the tribute list of Motecuhzoma Xocoyotzin. Pictured on this sheet is the biannual tribute due from the six towns of Xilotepec, an Otomi-speaking province northwest of the Valley of Mexico. Enumerated are women's skirts and blouses, men's mantles of various sorts, two warrior's costumes with shields, four wooden cribs filled with maize, beans, and other foodstuffs, and an eagle.

Gods'. Of these four offspring, the greatest was the Black Tezcatlipoca ('Smoking Mirror') of the north, the god of war and sorcery, and the patron deity of the royal house, to whom the new emperor prayed on his succession to office. He was everywhere, in all things, and could see into one's heart by means of his magic mirror. This, the 'real' Tezcatlipoca, was the giver and taker away of life and riches, and was much feared.

The White Tezcatlipoca of the west was the familiar Quetzalcoatl, the lord of life and the enemy of death. It was believed that the world had gone through four cosmic ages or Suns (like the Hindu *kalpas*), each destroyed by a cataclysm, and that this process of repeated creations and destructions was the result of the titanic struggle between the Black Tezcatlipoca and Quetzalcoatl, in each of which one or the other would be triumphant and would dominate the next age. The previous age perished in floods, and we ourselves live in the Fifth Sun, which was created at Teotihuacan when the last of the gods gathered there hurled himself in a great fire and rose up to the sky as the new sun. This age will be the final one, and is to be extinguished by earthquakes.

Central to the concepts of the Aztec destiny codified by Tlacaelel was the official cult of Huitzilopochtli, the Blue Tezcatlipoca of the south. The result of a miraculous birth from Coatlicue (an aspect of the female side of Ometeotl), he was the tutelary divinity of the Aztec people; the terrible warrior god of the Sun, he needed the hearts and blood of sacrificed human warriors so that he would rise from the east each morning after a nightly trip through the underworld.

On the east was the Red Tezcatlipoca, Xipe Totec 'Our Lord the Flayed One'. He was the god of spring and the renewal of the vegetation, impersonated by priests and those doing penance, wearing the skin of a flayed captive – the new skin symbolizing the 'skin' of new vegetation which the earth puts on when the rains come. At the end of twenty days the god-impersonator could take the skin off, but by this time he 'stank like a dead dog', as one source tells us.

Tlaloc was another nature god, the source of rain and lightning and thus central to their agricultural rites; he could also be quadruple, so that there were black, white, blue, and red Tlalocs, but he was generally depicted as blue-colored, with serpent-like fangs and goggles over the eyes. One of the more horrifying of Aztec practices was the mass sacrifice of small children on mountain tops to bring rain at the end of the dry season, in propitiation of Tlaloc. It was said that the more they cried, the more the Rain God was pleased. His cult yet survives among central Mexican peasants, although humans have probably not been sacrificed to him since early Colonial days.

The cults were presided over by a celibate clergy. Every priest had been to a seminary at which he was instructed in the complicated ritual which he was expected to carry out daily. Their long, unkempt hair clotted with blood, their ears and members shredded from self-mutilations effected with agave thorns and sting-ray spines, smelling of death and putrefaction, they must have been awesome spokesmen for the Aztec gods.

117   The daily life of all Aztecs was bound up with the ceremonies dictated by the machine-like workings of their calendar. The Almanac Year (*tonalpohualli*) of 260 days was the result of the intermeshing of 20 days (given names like Crocodile, Wind, House, Lizard, etc.) with the numbers 1 to 13, expressed in their books by dots only. To all individuals, each day in the *tonalpohualli* brought good or evil tidings in accordance with the prognostications of the priests; but the bad effects could be mitigated, so that if a child was born on an unfavorable day, his naming ceremony could be postponed to a better one. For each of the twenty 13-day 'weeks' there were special rites and presiding gods; there were also supernatural birds ruling over each of the 13 days of the 'week', and a constantly repeating series of 9 gods who reigned during the night.

The Solar Year was made up of 18 named months of 20 days each, with an unlucky and highly dangerous period of 5 extra days before the commencement of the next year. Again, every month had its own special ceremonies in which all the citizens of the capital participated; given this kind of cycle, it is hardly surprising that the months were closely correlated with the agricultural year, but there must have been a constant slippage in this respect since neither the Aztecs nor any other Mesoamericans used Leap Years or any other kind of intercalation to adjust for the fact that the true length of the year is a quarter-day longer than 365 days. The Solar Years were named after one of the four possible names of the Almanac Year which could fall on the last day of the eighteenth month, along with its accompanying numerical coefficient.

Observations of the sun, moon, planets, and stars were carried out by the Aztec priests, and apparently even by the rulers, but they were not so advanced in this respect as the Maya. After the sun, the most important heavenly body to the Aztecs was Venus, particularly in its first appearance, or heliacal rising, as Morning Star in the east, which they calculated took place every 584 days (the true figure is 583.92 days). While the Morning Star was thought to be the apotheosis of Topiltzin Quetzalcoatl, ruler of Tula, its heliacal rising was viewed as fraught with danger and they feared its rays at that time. It is a remarkable fact that every 104 Solar Years, all parts of their calendar coincided: the Almanac Year of 260 days, the Solar Year of 365 days, and the 584-day synodic period of Venus. It was impressed on the Aztec mind that this was a point at which the Fifth Sun could be destroyed, and all fires in every temple, palace, and household in the empire were extinguished. On the Hill of the Star, just east of Colhuacan in the Valley of Mexico, the Fire Priests anxiously watched to see if the Pleiades would cross the meridian at midnight on this date; if they did, then the universe would continue. A fire was kindled on fire-sticks in the newly opened breast of a captive, and the glowing embers were carried by runners to every part of the Aztec realm.

117 Schematic representation of the *tonalpohualli* or 260-day period of the Aztecs. The 20 named days intermesh with the numbers 1 to 13.

118 Page from the Codex Borgia, now in the Vatican Library. This, the finest of all Mexican manuscripts, might have been painted in Cholula, Puebla. The codex is of deerskin and is folded in screen fashion; it is 10.3 m long and 27 cm wide. The scene illustrates the dual aspect of existence, the Death God back-to-back with Quetzalcoatl, the Lord of Life. Around the edge of the page are various days from the 260-day count, one half assigned to the rule of one god and one half to the other. Mixteca–Puebla culture, Late Post-Classic period.

119 Page from the Codex Borgia. Depicted is the host of the night sky. Represented here, reading from left to right and from top to bottom, are Mixcoatl, the Milky Way; the Traveler of the Southern Sky; Xolotl, the planet Venus; the Traveler of the Northern Sky; the Moon Goddess, before moon; Tonatiuh, the Sun. Mixteca–Puebla culture, Late Post-Classic period.

All this complex information was recorded in folding-screen books of deerskin or agave paper, kept in the temples by the priests. The state archives also included economic accounts, maps, and, possibly, historical works. Curiously, no truly Aztec codices have survived the Conquest; the finest Post-Classic books which we have were painted in a place that with some confidence can be indicated as Cholula. But about the Aztec script we have some knowledge, for it definitely was of the rebus, 'puzzle-writing' sort; most frequently appearing were placenames, recorded so as to take advantage of common Nahuatl words: thus, the town 'Atlan' was written by combining pictographs of water (a-) and teeth (tlan-). Numbers up to 19 were expressed by dots, 20 by a flag, 400 by something like a pine tree, 8,000 by a pouch for holding copal incense – that is, the system was vigesimal, increasing in multiples of 20.

118
119

The ritual round must have provided year-long excitement and meaning to the life of the ordinary citizen of Tenochtitlan, with feasts, decoration of the idols, and dances and songs to the accompaniment of two-toned slit drums, upright drums, conch-shell trumpets, rattles, and flutes. Homage to the gods prescribed individual penances and burning of blood-spattered paper, burning of perfumed copal incense, and, most dramatically, immolation of thousands of human captives yearly. The victims themselves considered it a glorious death to be seized by the priests and stretched on their backs over a stone on the temple summit, an incision made in the chest with a flint knife, the heart ripped out and placed in the *cuauhxicalli*, or 'Eagle Vase', to be burned for the consumption of the gods. Quickly the corpse was decapitated and flayed.

The souls of warriors who had died under the sacrificial knife or on the field of battle went not to the Region of the Dead in the underworld, but directly to the Paradise of the Sun God, where they accompanied the celestial orb as beautiful hummingbirds. Curiously, so did the dread spirits of women who died in childbirth (for they also had fought their 'warrior' and lost) – it was their duty to rise up from the west each day to greet the sun at noon, conducting it into the nether regions. Others who likewise avoided extinction in Mictlan were those who had died in some manner connected with the Rain God: by lightning, drowning, or sufferers from dropsy and gout. They ascended to the Paradise of Tlaloc, where they spent an idyllic afterlife among flowers, butterflies, and other heavenly delights.

Most famous among the Aztec sacrifices was that of the handsome young captive annually chosen to impersonate the god Tezcatlipoca. For one year he lived a life of honor, worshipped literally as the embodiment of the deity; towards the end, he was given four beautiful maidens as his mistresses. Finally, he left them sadly, mounted the steps of the temple, smashing one by one the clay flutes on which he had played in his brief moment of glory, then was flung on his back so that the flint dagger might be plunged into his breast.

Aztec art and architecture were primarily ecclesiastical, rather than secular in nature. The leveling of the Sacred Precincts of

120 Sacrificial knife of flint with mosaic-incrusted handle in the form of an Eagle Knight. Late Post-Classic period. Length 30 cm.

121 Façade of Temple I, Malinalco, State of Mexico, a circular temple cut from the living rock. The work was carried out under orders from the Aztec emperors Ahuitzotl and Motecuhzoma Xocoyotzin, between AD 1501 and 1515 (in the Late Post-Classic period). The outer wall is now about 3 m high. Entrance to the interior was gained through a giant serpent face. Within can be seen an out-spread eagle in the center of the floor and above it a feline and other eagles stretched out on a circular banquette.

122 Colossal statue of Coatlicue, the old goddess of the earth and mother of gods and men. The head has been severed from the body, and two serpents rise from the neck, meeting to form a face. Her necklace is fashioned from human hearts and hands, with a pendant skull. The skirt is a web of writhing snakes. Since the goddess feeds on human corpses, her hands and feet are tipped with monstrous claws. Aztec, Late Post-Classic period. Ht 2.5 m.

Tenochtitlan and Tlatelolco by the Spaniards for their own administrative buildings, cathedral, and churches destroyed all but the foundations of the major Aztec temples, but some idea can be gained of their magnificence by those that remain elsewhere in the Valley of Mexico, such as the huge double temple at Tenayuca, or the wonderful rock-carved sanctuary at Malinalco, circular and therefore certainly sacred to Quetzalcoatl. To some eyes, Aztec sculpture may be repulsive and there is no doubt that the monumental figures of gods like Coatlicue may be terrifying, but there is no denying their awesome power. Power is also reflected in the more 'realistic' works such as the seated stone figure of Xochipilli ('Prince of Flowers'), the god of love and summertime, which continue traditions of workmanship perfected by the Toltecs. Or, in the same vein, the lovely sculptured drum from Malinalco, which recalls the Nahuatl war song:

> The earth shakes: the Mexica begins his song:
> He makes the Eagles and Jaguars dance with him!
> Come to see the Huexotzinca:

123 Statue of Xochipilli, the Aztec 'Prince of Flowers', patron god of dances, games, and love, and symbol of summertime. The god sits crosslegged on a temple platform which is adorned with a flower, butterflies, and clusters of four dots signifying the heat of the sun. He wears a mask and is decorated with hallucinogenic mushrooms and flowers from psychotropic plants, as well as with animal skins. Aztec, Late Post-Classic period. Ht of figure with base 1.2 m.

124 Carved wooden drum (*huehuetl*) from Malinalco, State of Mexico. The drum is carved in relief with scenes representing the 'Flowery', or Sacred, War of the Aztecs, symbolized by dancing eagles and jaguars, the sign 4 Motion (the present age of the world), and, as seen here in the upper register, the figure of the Sun as an eagle. Aztec, Late Post-Classic period. Ht 1.15 m.

> On the dais of the Eagle he shouts out,
> Loudly cries the Mexica.[10]

Aztec artisans in Tenochtitlan were arranged in an approximation of guilds and were famous for their fine work in feather mosaics; but they were hardly rivals to the great craftsmen of the Cholula area, who under influence from the Mixtecs in the south, Aztecs in the north, and possibly Tarascans in the west produced the magnificent Mixteca–Puebla style. Motecuhzoma himself would eat only from cups and plates of Cholula ware, and it is sure that much of the goldwork as well as practically all the fine masks and other ceremonial paraphernalia of wood encrusted with turquoise mosaic were also manufactured there. The stupendous collection of mosaic pieces once in the hands of Charles V and now in the British Museum, in Florence, and in Rome bears eloquent testimony to late Mexican workmanship in this medium, although most examples were consumed in the *pietre dure* 'laboratories' of Florence in the early nineteenth century.

Lastly something might be said of the mentality which enabled the Aztec people not only to survive misfortunes, disasters, and privations which would have broken others, but also to create one of the most advanced political states ever seen in Mexico. Raised in the most austere fashion in their homes and schools (education was universal and for both sexes), trained to withstand cold and hunger, Aztec individuals embodied ideals which would have done credit to an 'old Roman'. Self-restraint and humility were expected even of those whose fortunes soared, including the emperors themselves.

> The mature man:
> a heart as firm as stone,
> a wise countenance,
> the owner of a face, a heart,
> capable of understanding.[11]

125 Polychrome pottery cup, from Cholula, Puebla. Three jaguars prance around the exterior of the bowl. Mixteca–Puebla culture, Late Post-Classic period. Ht 12 cm.

Not for him the megalomaniac self-esteem and lust for riches exhibited to the Aztec disgust by the Spaniards!

Furthermore, as a curious foil to this optimistic dedication to war, sacrifice, and puritanical ideals there runs a singular streak of melancholy and pessimism in Aztec philosophy, a theme particularly developed by the closely allied Texcocan royal house. The transitoriness of life on this earth and the uncertainty of the hereafter appear in a song ascribed to King Nezahualcoyotl of Texcoco:

> Even jade is shattered,
> Even gold is crushed,
> Even quetzal plumes are torn . . .
> One does not live forever on this earth:
> We endure only for an instant![12]

Questions asked in a poem on the same theme:

> Will flowers be carried to the Kingdom of Death:
> Is it true that we are going, we are going?
> Where are we going, ay, where are we going?
> Will we be dead there or will we live yet?
> Does one exist again?[13]

are answered in another place:

> Perhaps we will live a second time?
> Thy heart knows:
> Just once do we live![14]

126 Aztec sculpture reflected in an obsidian mirror with carved wooden frame. Aztec, Late Post-Classic period. Diameter of frame 26 cm.

The Spanish Conquest

In the final ten years of the reign of Motecuhzoma Xocoyotzin, strange portents appeared to the terrified monarch. The first of these was a great comet 'like a tongue of fire, like a flame, as if showering the light of the dawn'. Then, in succession, a tower of the Great Temple burned mysteriously; the water of the lake foamed and boiled and flooded the capital; and a woman was heard crying in the night through the streets of Tenochtitlan. Two-headed men were discovered and brought to the ruler, but they vanished as soon as he looked at them. Worst of all, fisherfolk snared a bird like a crane, which had a mirror on its forehead; they showed it to Motecuhzoma in broad daylight, and when he gazed into the mirror, he saw the shining stars. Looking a second time, he saw armed men borne on the backs of deer. Consulting his soothsayers, they could tell him nothing, but Nezahualpilli, King of Texcoco, forecast the destruction of Mexico.

Inflicting great cruelties on his magicians for their inability to forestall the doom which he saw impending, the Aztec monarch was dumbfounded when an uncouth man arrived one day from the Gulf Coast and demanded to be taken into his presence. 'I come,' he announced, 'to advise you that a great mountain has been seen on the waters, moving from one part to the other, without touching the rocks.' Quickly clapping the wretch in jail, he despatched two trusted messengers to the coast to determine if this was so. When they returned they confirmed the story previously told, adding that strange men with white faces and hands and long beards had set off in a boat from 'a house on the water'. Secretly convinced that these were Quetzalcoatl and his companions, he had the sacred livery of the god and food of the land offered to them, which they immediately took back with them to their watery home, thus confirming his surmises. The gods had left some of their own foods in the form of sweet-tasting biscuits on the beach; the monarch ordered the holy wafers to be placed in a guilded gourd, covered with rich cloths, and carried by a procession of chanting priests to Tula of the Toltecs, where they were reverently interred in the ruins of Quetzalcoatl's temple.

The 'mountain that moved' was in reality the Spanish ship commanded by Juan de Grijalva, which after skirting the coast of Yucatan made the first Spanish landing on Mexican soil in the year 1518, near modern Veracruz. This reconnaissance was followed up in 1519 by the great armada that embarked from Cuba under the leadership of Hernán Cortés. In one of the terrible coincidences that history often deals out, it so happens that the Christian year 1519 was also the year 1 Reed in the Aztec calendar: the year in which Quetzalcoatl had been born, and the year in which his return from over the seas to the east of Mexico was foretold!

From the history of Prescott and in numberless romances many readers are familiar with the stirring events that led to the final death of the Aztec empire at the hands of Cortés. Briefly, the Aztec realm began to fall apart as soon as the conquerors landed, for many of the coastal peoples were only too glad to take the Spanish side against their oppressors. Backed by the advantages of horses, cannons, and huge war dogs, the like of which the Mexicans had never seen, and possessing an incredible fighting spirit, a relatively small band of men marched victoriously up into the highlands. After gaining as their allies the most deadly enemies of the Aztec state, the Tlaxcalans, the Spaniards were allowed by Motecuhzoma to walk into the great city of Tenochtitlan itself. He welcomed them as gods returning to their own homes and soon permitted himself to be kidnapped by them without resistance in the very heart of the city.

The powerless Motecuhzoma, alternating between fear and resignation to his own fate, died in the Spanish quarters during the great battle that ended with the invaders fleeing the city in the darkness on their way to the coast. It is not certain whether he was killed by Cortés or by the hands of his own people. His place was taken by Cuitlahuac, who reigned only four months, then by the great Cuauhtemoc (1521–24), who directed the fierce Aztec resistance to the returning Spaniards. Realizing full well that these foreigners were not gods as Motecuhzoma had thought, but implacable enemies bent on their total destruction, Cuauhtemoc held off both them and their bloodthirsty allies from Tlaxcala, fighting from rooftop to rooftop in the center of Tenochtitlan, but at a disadvantage against the brigantines which the Spaniards had built on the lake. The last and noblest of the Aztec emperors surrendered his besieged and starving city, its streets reeking with the stench of blood and corpses, on Wednesday, the 13th day of August in 1521. In the true tradition of Renaissance Spain, Cortés received him with honors, only to have him hanged three years later.

127 The Old World meets the New, AD 1519. Cortés and friendly nobles of the Tlaxcalan state. From the *Lienzo de Tlaxcala*.

Reigning monarchs of the Aztec state

Acamapichtli (1367–1387)
Huitzilihuitl (1391–1415)
Chimalpopoca (1415–1426)
Itzcoatl (1427–1440)
Motecuhzoma Ilhuicamina (1440–1468)
Axayacatl (1469–1481)
Tizoc (1481–1486)
Ahuitzotl (1486–1502)
Motecuhzoma Xocoyotzin (1502–1520)
Cuitlahuac (1520)
Cuauhtemoc (1521–1524)

Text references

With the exception of 6, which is reproduced by kind permission of the publishers, all references are to poems translated by the author from Spanish versions of the original Nahuatl texts.

1 M. León-Portilla, *Los Antiguos Mexicanos a través de sus Crónicas y Cantares*, pp. 21–2. Mexico 1961.
2 *Op. cit.*, p. 23.
3 *Op. cit.*, pp. 26–7.
4 A. M. Garibay, *Historia de la Literatura Náhuatl*, p. 316. Mexico 1953.
5 León-Portilla, *op. cit.*, p. 33.
6 Bernal, Díaz del Castillo, *The Discovery and Conquest of Mexico*. Routledge and Kegan Paul, London 1938.
7 León-Portilla, *op. cit.*, p. 63.
8 Garibay, *op. cit.*, p. 76.
9 Garibay, *op. cit.*, p. 215.
10 Garibay, *op. cit.*
11 León-Portilla, *op. cit.*, p. 147.
12 Garibay, *op. cit.*, p. 103.
13 M. León-Portilla, *Filosophía Náhuatl*, p. 57. Mexico 1956.
14 León-Portilla, *op. cit.*, p. 218.

Select bibliography

There has been no attempt to present here anything like an exhaustive coverage of Mexican archaeology, the titles of which run into many thousands. Rather, I have tried to guide the interested reader to those works which might be profitably consulted for further information; many of these publications themselves contain quite extensive bibliographies.

Chapter 1

The following can be unreservedly recommended as reliable surveys of Mesoamerica as a whole:

BRICKER, VICTORIA R., and JEREMY A. SABLOFF (eds). *Supplement to the Handbook of Middle American Indians*, vol. I: *Archaeology*. Austin, Texas, 1981. (An important updating of Wauchope 1964–1976.)

COVARRUBIAS, MIGUEL. *Indian Art of Mexico and Central America*. New York 1957.

KELLEY, JOYCE. *The Complete Visitor's Guide to Mesoamerican Ruins*. Norman, Oklahoma, 1982.

KIRCHHOFF, PAUL. 'Meso-America', in *Heritage of Conquest*, ed. Sol Tax, 17–30. Glencoe, Illinois, 1952.

MARQUINA, IGNACIO. *Arquitectura Prehispánica*. Mexico 1951.

SANDERS, WILLIAM T., and BARBARA J. PRICE. *Mesoamerica: the Evolution of a Civilization*. New York 1968.

WAUCHOPE, ROBERT (ed.). *Handbook of Middle American Indians*. Austin, Texas, 1964–1976. (A multi-volume series covering all aspects of life in Mesoamerica.)

WEAVER, MURIEL PORTER. *The Aztecs, Maya, and Their Predecessors*. 2nd edn, New York 1981.

Chapter 2

AVELEYRA ARROYO de ANDA, LUIS. 'The second mammoth and associated artifacts at Santa Isabel Iztapan, Mexico', *American Antiquity*, 22, no. 1 (1956), 12–28.

— 'The Primitive Hunters', in *Handbook of Middle American Indians*, vol. 1, ed. Robert Wauchope and Robert C. West, 384–412. Austin, Texas, 1964.

AVELEYRA ARROYO de ANDA, LUIS, and M. MALDONADO-KOERDELL. 'Association of artifacts with mammoths in the Valley of Mexico', *American Antiquity*, 18, no. 4 (1953), 332–40.

DE TERRA, HELMUT, JAVIER ROMERO, and T. DALE STEWART. *Tepexpan Man*. New York 1949.

FLANNERY, KENT V. 'The vertebrate fauna and hunting patterns', in *The Prehistory of the Tehuacan Valley*, vol. 1, *Environment and Subsistence*, ed. Douglas S. Byers, 132–177. Austin, Texas, 1967.

IRWIN-WILLIAMS, CYNTHIA. 'Summary of archaeological evidence from the Valsequillo region, Puebla, Mexico', in *Cultural Continuity in Mesoamerica*, ed. David Browman, 7–22. The Hague 1978.

MACNEISH, RICHARD S. 'Preliminary archaeological investigations in the Sierra de Tamaulipas, Mexico', *Transactions of the American Philosophical Society*, 48, pt 6 (1958).

Chapter 3

BYERS, DOUGLAS S., and RICHARD S. MACNEISH (gen. eds). *The Prehistory of the Tehuacan Valley*. 5 vols. Austin, Texas, 1967–77.

MACNEISH, RICHARD S. 'Preliminary archaeological investigations in the Sierra de Tamaulipas, Mexico', *loc. cit.*

MANGELSDORF, PAUL C. *Corn: Its Origin, Evolution and Improvement*. Cambridge 1974.

— 'The mystery of corn: new perspectives', *Proceedings of the American Philosophical Society*, 127, no. 4 (1983), 215–47.

NIEDERBERGER, CHRISTINE. 'Early sedentary economy in the Basin of Mexico', *Science*, 203 (1979), 131–2.

STARK, BARBARA L., and BARBARA VOORHIES (eds). *Prehistoric Coastal Adaptations: The Economy and Ecology of Maritime Middle America.* New York 1978.

Chapter 4

BELL, BETTY (ed.). *The Archaeology of West Mexico.* Ajijic, Jalisco, 1974.

COE, MICHAEL D. *The Jaguar's Children: Pre-Classic Central Mexico.* New York 1965.

DIXON, KEITH A. 'Ceramics from two Pre-classic periods at Chiapa de Corzo, Mexico', *Papers of the New World Archaeological Foundation*, no. 5. Orinda, California, 1959.

FLANNERY, KENT V. (ed.). *The Early Meso-american Village.* New York 1976.

FLANNERY, KENT V., JOYCE MARCUS, and STEPHEN A. KOWALEWSKI. 'The Preceramic and Formative of the Valley of Oaxaca', in *Supplement to the Handbook of Middle American Indians, loc. cit.*, 48–93. Austin, Texas, 1981.

FURST, PETER T. 'House of Darkness and House of Light', in *Death and the Afterlife in Pre-Columbian America*, ed. Elizabeth P. Benson, 33–68. Washington 1975.

HEIZER, ROBERT F., and JAMES A. BENNYHOFF. 'Archaeological investigation of Cuicuilco, Valley of Mexico', *Science*, 127, no. 3392 (1958), 232–3.

KAN, MICHAEL, CLEMENT MEIGHAN, and H. B. NICHOLSON. *Sculpture of Ancient West Mexico.* Los Angeles 1970.

PORTER, MURIEL N. *Tlatilco and the Pre-Classic Cultures of the New World.* New York 1953.

— 'Excavations at Chupícuaro, Guanajuato, Mexico', *Transactions of the American Philosophical Society*, 46, pt 5 (1956).

SOCIEDAD MEXICANA DE ANTHROPOLOGIA. *El Occidente de Mexico.* Mexico 1948.

TOLSTOY, PAUL, and LOUISE I. PARADIS. 'Early and Middle Preclassic culture in the Basin of Mexico', *Science*, 167 (1970), 344–51.

VAILLANT, GEORGE C. 'Excavations at Zacatenco', *Anthropological Papers of the American Museum of Natural History*, 32, pt 1. New York 1930.

— 'Excavations at El Arbolillo', *Anthropological Papers of the American Museum of Natural History*, 35, pt 2. New York 1935.

Chapter 5

BENSON, ELIZABETH P. (ed.). *Dumbarton Oaks Conference on the Olmec.* Washington 1968.

— (ed.). *The Olmec and Their Neighbors: Essays in Memory of Matthew W. Stirling.* Washington 1981.

BERNAL, IGNACIO. *The Olmec World.* Berkeley and Los Angeles 1967.

— 'The ball players of Dainzú', *Archaeology*, 21 (1968), 246–51.

CASO, ALFONSO. 'Calendario y escritura de las antiguas culturas de Monte Albán', in *Obras Completas*, Miguel Othón de Mendizabal, 6 vols., i, 113–45. Mexico, 1946–7.

COE, MICHAEL D. 'Cycle 7 monuments in Middle America', *American Anthropologist*, 59 (1957), 597–611.

— *America's First Civilization: Discovering the Olmec.* New York 1968.

COE, MICHAEL D., and RICHARD A. DIEHL. *In the Land of the Olmec.* 2 vols. Austin, Texas, 1980.

DRUCKER, PHILIP, ROBERT F. HEIZER, and ROBERT J. SQUIER. 'Excavations at La Venta, Tabasco, 1955', *Bureau of American Ethnology*, Bulletin 170. Washington 1959.

GROVE, DAVID C. 'The Olmec paintings of Oxtotitlan, Guerrero, Mexico', *Dumbarton Oaks Studies in Pre-Columbian Art and Archaeology*, no. 6. Washington 1970.

— *Chalcatzingo: Excavations on the Olmec Frontier.* London and New York 1984.

JORALEMON, PETER DAVID. 'A study of Olmec iconography', *Dumbarton Oaks Studies in Pre-Columbian Art and Iconography*, no. 7. Washington 1971.

— 'The Olmec Dragon: a study in Pre-Columbian iconography', in *Origins of Religious Art and Iconography in Preclassic Mesoamerica*, ed. H. B. Nicholson, 27–71. Los Angeles 1976.

SOUSTELLE, JACQUES. *The Olmec.* New York and London 1984.

STIRLING, MATTHEW W. 'An Initial Series from Tres Zapotes, Vera Cruz, Mexico', *National Geographic Society, Contributed Technical Papers*, i, no. 1. Washington 1940.

STIRLING, MATTHEW W. 'Stone monuments of southern Mexico', *Bureau of American Ethnology*, Bulletin 138. Washington 1943.

Chapter 6

Teotihuacan civilization:

LINNÉ, SIGVALD. *Archaeological Researches at Teotihuacan, Mexico.* Stockholm 1934.

— *Mexican Highland Cultures.* Stockholm 1942.

MILLER, ARTHUR G. *The Mural Painting of Teotihuacan.* Washington 1973.

MILLON, RENÉ. *Urbanization at Teotihuacan, Mexico.* Austin, Texas, 1973–. (So far the

first two volumes presenting the maps and their interpretation have appeared.)
— 'Teotihuacan: city, state, and civilization', in *Supplement to the Handbook of Middle American Indians, loc. cit.*, 198–243. Austin, Texas, 1981.
SANDERS, WILLIAM T., JEFFREY R. PARSONS, and ROBERT S. SANTLEY. *The Basin of Mexico: Ecological Processes in the Evolution of a Civilization*. New York 1979.
SEJOURNÉ, LAURETTE. *Un Palacio en la Ciudad de los Dioses, Teotihuacan*. Mexico 1959.

Cholula, Cacaxtla and Xochicalco:
CASO, ALFONSO. 'Calendario y escritura de Xochicalco', in *Los Calendarios Prehispánicos*, 166–86. Mexico 1967.
HIRTH, KENNETH G. 'Transportation architecture at Xochicalco, Morelos, Mexico', *Current Anthropology*, 23, no. 3 (1982), 322–4.
LOPEZ de M., DIANA, and DANIEL MOLINA F. *Cacaxtla, Guía Oficial*. Mexico 1980.
MARQUINA, IGNACIO (coordinator). *Proyecto Cholula*. Mexico 1970.
SÁENZ, CESAR A. 'Xochicalco, Temporada 1960'. *Instituto Nacional de Antropología e Historia, Colección Informes*, no. 11. Mexico 1962.

Cultures of the Gulf Coast:
DRUCKER, PHILIP. 'The Cerro de las Mesas offering of jade and other materials', *Bureau of American Ethnology*, Bulletin 157, 25–68. Washington 1955.
GARCÍA PAYÓN, JOSÉ. 'El Tajín', Guía Oficial, *Instituto Nacional de Antropología e Historia*. Mexico 1957.
KAMPEN, MICHAEL E. *The Sculptures of El Tajín, Veracruz, Mexico*. Gainesville, Florida, 1972.
MEDELLÍN ZENIL, ALFONSO. *Cerámicas del Totonacapan*. Xalapa, Veracruz 1960.
PROSKOURIAKOFF, TATIANA. 'Varieties of Classic Central Veracruz Sculpture', *Carnegie Institution of Washington, Contributions to American Anthropology and History*, no. 58. Washington 1954.
STIRLING, MATTHEW W. 'Stone monuments of southern Mexico', *Bureau of American Ethnology*, Bulletin 138. Washington 1943.

Classic Monte Albán:
BLANTON, RICHARD E. *Monte Albán: Settlement Patterns at the Ancient Zapotec Capital*. New York 1978.
CASO, ALFONSO. *Las Estelas Zapotecas*. Mexico 1928.
CASO, ALFONSO, and IGNACIO BERNAL. *Urnas de Oaxaca*. Mexico 1952.
PADDOCK, JOHN (ed.). *Ancient Oaxaca*. Stanford, California 1966.

Chapter 7

ACOSTA, JORGE R. 'Interpretación de algunos de los datos obtenidos en Tula relativos a la época tolteca', *Revista Mexicana de Estudios Antropológicos*, 14, pt 2, 75–110. Mexico 1956–7.
DAVIES, NIGEL. *The Toltecs until the Fall of Tula*. Oklahoma 1977.
DIEHL, RICHARD A. *Tula, the Toltec Capital of Ancient Mexico*. London and New York 1983.
DI PESO, CHARLES C. 'Archaeology and ethnohistory of the northern Sierra', *Handbook of Middle American Indians*, vol. 4, ed. Robert Wauchope, 3–25. Austin, Texas, 1966.
DUTTON, BERTHA P. 'Tula of the Toltecs', *El Palacio*, 62, nos. 6–7, 195–251. Santa Fé 1955.
JIMÉNEZ MORENZO, WIGBERTO. 'Síntesis de la historia precolonial del Valle de México', *Revista Mexicana de Estudios Antropológicos*, 14, pt 1, 219–36. Mexico 1954–5.
KELLEY, J. CHARLES. 'Archaeology of the northern frontier: Zacatecas and Durango', in *Handbook of Middle American Indians*, vol. 11, ed. Robert Wauchope, Gordon F. Ekholm, and Ignacio Bernal, 768–801. Austin, Texas, 1971.
KIRCHHOFF, PAUL. 'Quetzalcoatl, Huemac y el fin de Tula', *Cuadernos Americanos*, 84, 163–96. Mexico 1955.

Chapter 8

BURGOA, FR. FRANCISCO de. *Geográfica Descripción*, 2 vols. Mexico 1934. (Contains an account of Mitla.)
CASO, ALFONSO. *Interpretation of the Codex Bodley*. Mexico 1960.
— 'Mixtec writing and calendar', in *Handbook of Middle American Indians*, vol. 3, pt 2, ed. Robert Wauchope, 948–61. Austin, Texas, 1965.
— *El Tesoro de Monte Albán*. Memorias del Instituto Nacional de Antropología e Historia 3. Mexico 1969.
Relación de Michoacan (1541). Transcription, prologue, introduction, and notes by José Tudela. Madrid 1956.
SMITH, MARY ELIZABETH. *Picture Writing from southern Mexico: Mixtec place signs and maps*. Norman, Oklahoma, 1973.

SPORES, RONALD. *The Mixtec Kings and Their People*. Norman, Oklahoma, 1967.

van ZANTWIJK, R. A. M. *Servants of the Saints, the Social and Cultural Identity of a Tarascan Community in Mexico*. Assen, Netherlands, 1967.

Chapter 9

The literature on the Aztecs is enormous. The really important works on the subject were written either not long after the Conquest, or else in the Colonial period by scholars with access to early records. Of all sources, the monumental encyclopedia by Sahagún stands supreme, since it is based upon materials written in Nahuatl in the mid-sixteenth century. Regarding the Conquest of Mexico, no account could be more exciting and readable than that of Bernal Díaz del Castillo, who was an eyewitness to the actual events.

BARLOW, R. H. 'The extent of the empire of the Culhua Mexica', *Ibero-Americana*, 28. Berkeley and Los Angeles 1949.

CASO, ALFONSO. *The Aztecs, People of the Sun*. Norman, Oklahoma, 1958.

CORTÉS, HERNÁN. *The Letters of Cortés to Charles V*. Translated by Francis A. Mac-Nutt. 2 vols. New York and London 1908.

DAVIES, NIGEL. *The Aztecs, A History*. New York 1973.

DÍAZ del CASTILLO, BERNAL. *The True History of the Conquest of New Spain*. Translated by A. P. Maudslay. London 1908–16. (American edition, New York 1958.)

KIRCHHOFF, PAUL. 'Land tenure in ancient Mexico'. *Revista Mexicana de Estudios Antropológicos*, 14, pt 1, 351–62. Mexico 1954–5.

LEÓN-PORTILLA, MIGUEL. *Los Antiguos Mexicanos a través de sus Crónicas y Cantares*. Mexico 1961.

— *Aztec Thought and Culture*. Norman, Oklahoma, 1963.

LINNÉ, SIGVALD. *El Valle y la Ciudad de México en 1550*. Stockholm 1948.

NICHOLSON, HENRY B. 'Religion in Pre-Hispanic central Mexico', in *Handbook of Middle American Indians*, vol. 10, ed. Robert Wauchope, Gordon F. Ekholm, and Ignacio Bernal, 395–446. Austin, Texas, 1971. (The essential work on Aztec religion.)

— 'Revelation of the Great Temple', *Natural History*, 91, no. 7 (1982), 48–58.

PASZTORY, ESTHER. *Aztec Art*. New York 1983.

SAHAGÚN, FRAY BERNADINO de. *General History of the Things of New Spain*. Translation from the Nahuatl by Arthur J. O. Anderson and Charles E. Dibble. Santa Fé 1950–69. (A massive scholarly encyclopedia of almost all aspects of Aztec life by its greatest student. Book 12 presents an absorbingly interesting account of the Conquest from the native point of view.)

SOUSTELLE, JACQUES. *The Daily Life of the Aztecs*. New York 1962.

van ZANTWIJK, RUDOLF. 'Principios organizadores de los mexicas, una introducción del sistema interno del régimen azteca', *Estudios de Cultura Nahuatl*, vol. IV, 187–222. Mexico 1963.

List of illustrations

All maps and drawings are by Dr Patrick Gallagher, unless otherwise indicated.

Frontispiece: Monument 1, San Lorenzo, Veracruz. Photo courtesy Matthew W. Stirling and the National Geographic Society.

1 Map of major topographical features of Mesoamerica.
2 Central highlands of Mexico, near Puebla. Photo Michael D. Coe.
3 *Chinampas* in the vicinity of Xochimilco, Valley of Mexico. Photo Michael D. Coe.
4 Chart of cultural periods and changes of climate in Mexico.
5 Native language groups of Mexico.
6 Sites of the Early Hunters and Archaic periods.
7 Clovis point from the Weicker Ranch, Durango. Based on J. L. Lorenzo, 'A fluted point from Durango, Mexico' (fig. 141).
8 Animal head carved from the sacrum of an extinct camelid. Photo courtesy Instituto Nacional de Antropología e Historia, Mexico.
9 Fossil human skull from Tepexpan, Valley of Mexico. Photo courtesy Instituto Nacional de Antropología e Historia.

Index

Numerals in *italics* refer to illustration numbers